Praise for *The Generosity Path*

Mark Ewert has written *The Generosity Path* with an abundance of kindness and grace. It is one of those rare books that creates a shared journey between the author and his readers. We never feel alone as Ewert explores the underlying currents that connect charitable giving to living out a set of values and beliefs, while we develop an intentional spiritual practice.

Ewert provides a framework for readers to free themselves of unreasonable fears about poverty and from unrealistic fantasies about wealth. He awakens the slumbering philanthropist in us by providing tools to help us become part of a generous community. He reflects on ways in which we are already generous and helps us find ways to expand our generosity, no matter our life circumstances.

The Generosity Path has earned a spot at the top of my recommended list of spiritual stewardship resources. I will purchase multiple copies while recommending it to both individuals and communities of practice. This book is for everyone who has the desire to become intentionally generous amidst a quagmire of consumerism.

—Wayne B. Clark, author of *Beyond Fundraising:*
The Complete Guide to Congregational Stewardship

This book shows that being a philanthropist is often more connected to a way of thinking than it is to simply being wealthy. It offers concrete and easy-to-implement steps to make the mindset shift from being a donor to becoming a philanthropist.

—Phyllis R. Caldwell, former president, Washington Area
Women's Foundation

Mark Ewert's *The Generosity Path* walks readers through a process of creating purpose in their lives. The activities and journaling suggestions that end each chapter provide welcome opportunities for readers to take steps along the generosity path with Mark at their side. If generosity is about being authentically present with other people and leveraging the fellowship of community, then Mark has given his readers a real gift through the personal experience and curated stories he shares so eloquently here in this book.

> —David Greene, vice president, Bernstein Global Wealth Management, and author of *Dollars and Sense: Ten Fundamentals of Financial Success*

Giving is a sacred act. It situates the giver and the recipient in moral and spiritual traditions that stretch back thousands of years. Working from this premise gives Mark Ewert's account of generosity a depth that many others lack. And though he doesn't shrink from discussing the more technical and practical aspects of giving, these never overwhelm what is essentially a beautiful act that has meanings far beyond those understood by donor and recipient. These acts of generosity have remade our world and have the promise of making it even better.

I'm especially grateful for the care that Ewert takes to embed generosity in the daily round, in the concrete give and take of everyday decisions, in the time we give ourselves to stop and reflect. Each chapter provides practical exercises to help one or another aspect of generosity come alive. These exercises include a generosity self-assessment, journaling suggestions, and other practices that help transform giving from an object of study to a way of thinking and being.

> —G. Albert Ruesga, president and CEO, Greater New Orleans Foundation

Generosity is not only a sign of spiritual growth, but a path toward wholeness and maturity. Using not only his own experience, but also interviews with twelve generous people, Mark Ewert maps out a path that all of us can walk. Whether you read this book alone or, better, in a small group, you will be enriched by the true generosity of spirit within.

—Rev. Dr. John A. Buehrens, co-author of *A Chosen Faith: An Introduction to Unitarian Universalism*

Inspiring, sensitive, and encouraging, *The Generosity Path* invites the reader, gently and clearly, into a deeper practice of giving. This wonderful book should be read by anyone who cares about living their life with meaning and purpose and who wants to contribute to more justice and love in the world.

—Rev. Dr. Rebecca Parker, president and professor of theology, Starr King School for the Ministry

The Generosity Path

The Generosity Path

Finding the Richness in Giving

Mark V. Ewert

Skinner House Books
Boston

www.skinnerhouse.org

Printed in the United States

Cover and text design by Suzanne Morgan
Author photo by Michael K. Wilkinson

Print ISBN: 978-1-55896-716-8
eBook ISBN: 978-1-55896-717-5

6 5 4 3 2 1
15 14 13

Library of Congress Cataloging-in-Publication Data
Ewert, Mark V.
The generosity path : finding the richness in giving / Mark V. Ewert.
  pages cm
  Includes bibliographical references.
  ISBN 978-1-55896-716-8 (pbk. : alk. paper)—
  ISBN 978-1-55896-717-5 (ebook) 1. Generosity—Economic aspects. 2.
Gifts—Economic aspects. I. Title.
  BJ1533.G4E94 2013
  177'.7—dc23
                        2013019996

We gratefully acknowledge permission to reprint "Posthumous" by Jean Nordhaus, reprinted by permission of The Ohio State University Press; "Benediction" by Rebecca Parker, co-author of *Saving Paradise and Proverbs of Ashes* and author of *Blessing the World*, reprinted by permission of author; "Though I may give all I possess…" by Hal Hopson, from *Though I May Speak With Bravest Fire (The Gift of Love)* by Hal Hopson © 1972 Hope Publishing Co., Carol Stream, IL 60188, all rights reserved, used by permission; the lines from "Natural Resources", copyright © 2002 by Adrienne Rich, copyright © 1978 by W.W. Norton & Company, Inc., from *The Fact of a Doorframe: Selected Poems 1950–2001* by Adrienne Rich, used by permission of W.W. Norton & Company, Inc.

Dedicated to Steven, for his love and exquisite support.
And to the generous people who shared their stories with me.

Contents

Your Gifts

Your gifts
whatever you discover them to be
can be used to bless or curse the world.
The mind's power,
    The strength of the hands,
        The reaches of the heart,
the gift of speaking, listening, imagining, seeing, waiting,
Any of these can serve to feed the hungry,
    bind up wounds,
    welcome the stranger,
    praise what is sacred,
    do the work of justice
        or offer love.
Any of these can draw down the prison door
    hoard bread,
    abandon the poor,
    obscure what is holy,
    comply with injustice
        or withhold love.

You must answer this question:
What will you do with your gifts?
Choose to bless the world.

—Rebecca Ann Parker

Introduction

Welcome to the generosity path. No matter who you are, and more likely because of who you are, I am glad to have you join me on this path for a while, as I have spent many years finding my way to this purpose.

The concept of generosity presented here includes giving and receiving. Sometimes when something is given skillfully from one person to another, it is hard to distinguish who gains the most—giver or receiver. For this reason, throughout the book they are sometimes hard to separate. Giving sheds light on being a recipient; receiving informs being a giver. Through these interactions, they encourage and fuel each other.

The book is designed to enrich your experience and understanding of how to skillfully grow your giving to make a bigger difference in the world. As you read examples of how others have learned about generosity, and consider your own learning, I hope the examples will shed light on how you might guide others on their way as well. To that end, I include information about ways to teach generosity. Because giving naturally builds connections between people, this may lead to fellowship on this path, either in a community of which you are already a part, one you find, or create. Being part of a community that supports and prompts generousness adds dimensions of engagement that would otherwise not be possible.

Generosity can have many expressions, including care, time, skill, intelligence, gifts, and money. I believe that one cannot omit any of these without curtailing them all. Financial generosity is one of the most challenging expressions, and perhaps holds the most opportunity to make a difference in the world and our own well-being. For that reason, this book emphasizes financial generosity. Once you have become grounded, thoughtful, educated, and strategic with your financial generosity, you might be called a *philanthropist*. The word *philanthropy* comes from the Greek *philanthropia*. Broken down into its parts, it translates to *phil*—"loving"—and *anthropos*—"mankind." Therefore: loving or useful to mankind. In my use of the word, you do not need to be rich or have a big stash of money to give away in order to be a philanthropist. This updating of the term—and restoring more of its original meaning—applies, no matter what form or scale your generosity takes. If you don't already consider yourself a philanthropist, I hope that you will by the time you finish this book and do the practices included here.

The intelligence for this book comes from a number of sources. One is a set of interviews with people who were referred to me as generous; these provide a lot of anecdotal information and some inspiring stories. Another source is quotes and comments from people, some of them well-known, who have considered and written about generosity from the perspective of philosophy, religion, social change, and history. I also drew from research in behavioral economics and other fields of study. Much of the content emerged from my professional, volunteer, and personal experience with people who are contemplating their financial giving—and the organizations to which they give.

A brief word about my background. Because of who I am and my history, my greatest opportunities for personal growth seem to be in learning to be more open-hearted and open-handed—more generous. For many years I worked as a fundraiser for a national nonprofit. Early on, my job involved teaching people to ask their friends and family for charitable donations to the cause. (Note: "charitable donation" is an American tax-related term meaning a gift, usually financial, to an Internal Revenue Service-qualified not-for-profit organization that has a religious, educational, literary, charitable, or scientific purpose. In this use, the term is far removed from the word "charity," which has its own set of associations.) Later, I provided internal support and consultation to regional and local offices in various parts of the country. I helped them with their fundraising strategy, training their staff members, developing their materials, and sometimes with making financial requests of families or corporations for large charitable contributions.

Onsite staff members would take advantage of my support and presence to have me ask a family for a large gift, one much larger than they had ever previously requested. During a typical meeting like this, after we had been introduced and exchanged pleasantries, settled in and discussed what was needed and why, I would make the request for a sizable donation. Those moments between when I made the request, the donor considered it, and they gave an answer were often silent and breathless, engaging and intense. There was always the sense that people were considering profound topics when formulating an answer. In fact, many of these families had lost a loved one or lived with a legacy of disease that had affected many family members. Perhaps they were remembering lost relatives or wondering

> Giving brings happiness at every stage of its expression. We experience joy in forming the intention to be generous; we experience joy in the actual act of giving something; and we experience joy in remembering the fact we have given.
>
> Lama Surya Das,
> quoting the Buddha

about what their wishes might have been, had they been present. Maybe they were just considering their own financial wherewithal. If they said yes, I felt that they were giving far more than money and gaining far more than a tax deduction. The connection to the organization, its mission, and activities, was helping those families bring meaning to their lives—holding the family together, memorializing someone, making a concrete gesture of support for someone struggling with illness, or just making a difference in the part of the world they cared most about. Much of this was unspoken, but it was beautiful and spirit-filled.

I learned a lot during those meetings. As a fundraiser, I learned that asking people for money could be a service I provided to those donors; one they would welcome and accept with gratitude, and one that could have a transformative effect on them. I also learned that for a donor, reaching out to the edge of your generosity to make a gift could be honoring, restorative, and energizing—and it could lend purpose to your life. These experiences made me dissatisfied with the more common fundraising activities—the mailing of return-address labels, the galas and auctions, the 5K races, the high-donor cocktail parties, the exchange for tote bags or travel mugs. All of those might be useful to publicize the nonprofit and engage people at modest giving levels, but the magic and deep change happened when the big, challenging requests were considered.

> Every time I take a step in the direction of generosity, I know that I am moving from fear to love.
>
> Henri J.M. Nouwen

During that time, I joined All Souls, a Unitarian Universalist church in my home community of Washington DC, and started volunteering to help raise funds for their mission—what we call *stewardship*. That allowed me to explore the rich underlying currents that connect charitable giving to living out a set of values and beliefs, and developing a spiritual practice. It also gave me a place to center my practice of generosity, both financially (as I have given more to that church than any other charity) and with my time, presence, intelligence, and muscle. My church is my spiritual home, my central community. We do wonderful social-justice work—in political organizing, advocacy, and direct service—and we try to live according to our shared values. All Souls has served as an incubator, a substantial support, and a community of practice for my generosity work.

I have expanded this mission work over the past five years as a consultant for religious organizations, to help build communities of stewards. I have come to understand the challenges and benefits of being intentionally generous in a community setting. This book reflects those challenges and benefits. Doing some of this work on your own is essential, especially at the beginning, to create a strong foundation for further work and clear direction. However, working as part of a community brings an additional set of dynamics that are exciting and supportive, challenging in their own ways, and full of new potentials.

There are legions of generous people in every community. Despite this, I have walked the generosity path alone at times. This is partly due to the nature of this undertaking, which is deeply personal; one must do some of this work internally. Yet it is also because most of our cultural messages around money support the opposite trajectory—toward stockpiling, improving our social status, and counteracting our daily stress by spending for our own comfort, even on things that are not good for our health and well-being. That is why I am trying to get people like you to join me on this path. I have found people who have walked this way before me, to see what they learned along the way and to discover where they ended up. I hope I can drop crumbs and leave signposts as I go so that others can find their way as well. This is a book of crumbs and, I hope, some signposts.

A Note on the Interviews

This book contains stories and quotes from ten in-person interviews. These real-life stories help illuminate the path as you step into more intentional generosity. Eight of the interviews are with individuals; two are with married couples.

After teaching a course on generosity with my good friend and colleague Sharon Groves, I asked each of the participants to suggest someone whom they knew personally and consider extremely generous. Most of the people they suggested I had never met before. I contacted each person, let them know I had been referred by their friend, and asked for some time to do the interview.

In each case, the people were gracious and gave as much time as needed for the lengthy interviews, although all were initially puzzled and some were embarrassed about why they had been identified as generous. I used the same set of questions for each interview, yet their stories and answers led us to different discussion areas each time. The questions themselves can be found on page 122, with some suggestions about how you might use them yourself.

Each story is true, although some minor details have been omitted or changed. I changed the names of the interviewees to protect their personal information and stories. As you will see, each person honored me with being frank about their history, present situation, and hopes for the future. They were inspiring gifts to me, and I pass those gifts on to you. As the purpose is neither exposé nor glorification, what each conveys with honesty is more important than her or his exact identity.

The interviewees are a diverse group. Some were raised with wealth and some in relative poverty. Some came from families, or later had mentors, who taught them about generosity and how to be charitable. Some of them developed this capacity entirely on their own. This raises some questions about where generosity comes from and how one might teach it. This topic is covered in chapter 3, and I hope you will reflect on your own biography in this way.

Journaling

Each chapter ends with activities and journaling suggestions for self-reflection. Please consider taking time for these elements, as they engage you where you are. Feel free to adapt them to your needs and situation.

Self-reflection is an essential tool of experiential learning. If you are not familiar with it, it may seem dull or awkward at first, or pointless because no one else will be reading it. A journal is not a diary; you are not merely recounting the happenings of the day. To get beyond merely chronicling events, consider writing about yourself from an outsider's perspective—as if you are observing yourself. Include stories and give a good amount of detail. This will provide context later if you choose to review what you have written.

A journal also is a good place to speculate about why something may be happening, or to formulate a potential resolution to something you are considering. This invites more gathering of information to enrich your conjectures. When journaling, you can give your judgments free reign. Although you might not want to judge circumstances, other people, or yourself, your journal can be a private place to ponder and adjust your own opinions.

I suggest getting a paperback-sized spiral-bound notebook specifically for this purpose. You may want to carry it with you and make notes while you are out in public or at work. Before each journaling session, settle yourself somewhere comfortable. Take a few deep breaths to get centered, and contemplate the topic for a few minutes before starting to write.

Small-Group Discussion Guide

At the back of this book you will find a small-group discussion guide. It is geared toward the potential leaders. It includes eleven sessions, one for each chapter, plus a closing session. A book club or other small group you're already part of would be an ideal situation. If you belong to a community that has a system for small-group discussion, you may be able to just suggest this topic within that program. If you belong to a community that does not usually facilitate small groups, this might be an opportunity to get to know a group of people better—yet it may require some recruiting on your part. If you are in a situation where you are on your own, you can still use the guide along with your journal to enrich your progress.

While reading this book, challenge yourself to be open-minded and open-hearted. If something makes you uncomfortable or puzzled, that may be a sign that you have come upon an opportunity, which will warrant slowing down. You may benefit most from reflecting on your reactions and staying with the content until it becomes clearer.

CHAPTER 1

Starting Where You Are

The word *generous* comes from the Latin *generosus*, which means "noble, magnanimous." *Magnanimous,* in turn, comes from the Latin words *magnu*—"great"—and *animus*—"soul." According to the Oxford English Dictionary (OED), *generous* means "freely giving more than is necessary or expected." So generosity includes the idea of open-handedness, along with a connection to our internal experience and spirituality. We can apply the concept very broadly to encompass how we treat each other everywhere: on the street or at distant locations, to create connections with people we do not know, and to weave a community of care with our friends and loved ones.

Generosity's rich meaning can inspire us. It implies giving *freely,* so the giver holds choice and control—and freedom always feels good. It is about giving *more than necessary,* so it is not limited by being required or indispensable. It is *more than expected,* so it goes beyond the obligation to give or what is anticipated by the recipient. Finally, generosity *ennobles* us; it makes us *great souls.* Who would not want to feel that they are a generous person? Compare this to words such as *charity, alms,* and *aid,* which label the recipient as poor; *donation* and *contribution,* which are cold, technical terms; and *grant,* which is formal legalese. *Philanthropy* is a wonderful word in its Greek origins ("loving human-kind"), yet it has come to imply a rare few who have the wealth and power to be *philanthropists.* It's time to redefine the term *philanthropist* and make it available to everyone, regardless of their resources. You—no matter your level of income, savings, or financial worth—can be a philanthropist.

As an added delight, the prefix of generosity, *gen*, means "birth." This prefix is also used in *generative*, which the *OED* tells us means "relating to or capable of production or reproduction." So generosity causes something new to be produced—either a connection between people or between people and organizations. These ideas of generativity—passage, growth, and connection—form the basis for the title of this book. It is designed to help you envision a journey that you create, and that helps you to develop.

This journey has benefits in addition to your development. Research by the University of British Columbia and Harvard Business School shows that spending money on someone else—as little as $5 a day—can significantly boost your happiness.[1] Students who practiced random acts of kindness were significantly happier than those who were not given this task.[2] In another study, college students were given money and directed to either spend it on themselves or spend it prosocially (on activities meant to benefit other people). Participants who spent it prosocially were happier at the end of the day than those who spent it on themselves. Henry (see page 136) points to the motivating effect of good feelings, as well as the advantage of learning from giving. "When giving, in addition to feeling good about it, you are also receiving something valuable—so getting involved is a learning process. That is pretty obvious to me now."

As you develop your intelligence and facility to give and receive, you may find that your passion for it grows. That is what has happened for Amy-Lee (p. 108). This is how she states it:

> You have to make a lot of choices in life; at a certain point you have to decide what is really important and then really get behind it. It is beyond, *it would be nice*; it is like more like, *what is the hold up, why aren't you doing something?* That voice has gotten louder and louder over time.

The generosity path incorporates all forms of generosity, being open-handed and open-hearted with all of types of resources: time, money, intelligence, skill, muscle, and material goods. Examples and information about each of these are presented throughout this book. However, the primary focus is financial generosity. This is because money carries greater meaning and power in people's consciousness. People frequently fantasize about wealth or fear poverty, no matter their economic status. Even in families, parents withhold information about their resources from their children. Friends may not share anything about their finances with each other, let alone how they decide how much money to give charitably, and to whom. As Barbara (p. 6) puts it, "It is not so much about money, which is almost embarrassing to talk about. I guess I am generous of spirit, if that is the phrase; it is part of what I am." In addition, the dynamic of "having" and others "not-having," and what can be done about it, troubles many people. It may fill us with guilt and shame, no matter which side of this line we find ourselves.

> Even after all this time
> The sun never says to the earth
> "you owe me."
> Look what happens with a
> Love like that!
> — It lights the whole Sky.
>
> Hafiz

Also, some people hold money separately, cordoned off in a distinct category. It is as if they have created an equation or bargain, where they must either give time or money. Some behavioral economics research on this idea, called the "substitution effect," has shown this to be true. When researcher Jonathan Gruber studied the effect of tax policy on giving, he found that people who gave financially to religious institutions tended to participate less.[3] Sometimes circumstances dictate that the capacity to volunteer may increase when one has more time than money; the reverse also can be true. Research also shows that potential contributors consider *volunteering* differently than their financial giving. They see monetary donations as supporting the work of others and depending on one's financial wherewithal.[4] Liz (p. 174) expresses this well: "I don't have a lot of money, my family does not have a lot of money, but we do have a lot of time and energy and creativity and love. That is what generosity is for us."

Despite the research and the above quotation, other evidence suggests the opposite—that involvement can encourage financial donation, and giving monetarily can encourage volunteering. The people I interviewed followed both these paths and research shows that volunteering allows potential donors to assess the good use of their contributions.[5]

Daniel is a powerful example of this (p. 70). He had been a busy and stressed professional with little time, so he increased his financial giving because he had the capacity to do so. He said, "We were writing big checks, but there was no interaction with people— with people who provided services or people who needed services." Dissatisfaction with this led him to devote his life to full-time volunteer service. He now gives more moderately because of that shift. During both phases he was generous, in accordance with his resources at the time. Daniel's story reminds us that when people dedicate their time to service professions, which tend to be less well-compensated, it affects their finances. This may be true for Liz, who, due to her work overseas, may have unusual expenses and may not be building retirement savings and equity in a home in America.

The generosity path can help people become more generous with both their time *and* money in relation to their resources. As Elise, who, with her husband, adopted a son and started a nonprofit (p. 56), states, "Not just with money but also with giving someone love or a hug or help, be more responsive in your giving for whatever that person needs." Although financial generosity may present more of a challenge for many people, it will also afford a greater opportunity for personal growth, a feeling of internal alignment, and perhaps even spiritual development.

Do not discount care and financial giving within your family. We may find it easier to be generous with them, or we may consider it our duty. Yet, the unconditional and lifelong nature of family care puts special demands on us. A lifetime of intimacy and sharing of resources will inevitably include times when we are not as mature or altruistic as we might like to be. Being recognized as magnanimously generous may be easier with people we see less frequently and in more public settings. Given the quantity and quality of our giving to family members, this must be considered an aspect of generosity.

As you embark upon the generosity path, also consider your own self-care. This does not mean self-indulgence or personal entitlement, i.e., what you crave or feel you deserve. Self-care is necessary for generosity because if you are balanced and well-grounded, you are more apt and able to give. Barry, Elise's husband (p. 56), states this frankly: "When I am feeling wealthy and secure, I am quite generous. When I am not feeling secure, I am not."

This book emphasizes the care of those who are in need. Your personal giving focus may be on environmental causes, cultural giving in the arts, education, or other issues. It will be up to you to choose your own mission. We share responsibility in all these areas, which provide broader benefit to humanity. This book focuses on the survival needs of people because they can be most urgent, and the giving to help them more direct. It also references religious ideas and practices, which are a rich and well-developed resource for reflection in generosity. Many stories in this book give examples of giving to religious institutions. This is meant neither to bias your consideration of where you might exercise your generosity, nor to encourage you to ascribe to any particular belief system.

Your intuition and emotions will guide you in the direction your generosity should take. Your intellect and reason also will support you in being more generous. We cannot as individuals solve all of the world's problems, and our resources have limits. We must make choices about what to do, the kind of change we want to make in the world. For some, that mission will come from personal experience, from something that involves a loved one, or it may be something that moves them so much that they have to
text continues on page 8

BARBARA

I believe very strongly in the necessity of being good to other people.

—Barbara

It is hard to tell Barbara's age; she has young-adult children and is probably nearing a normal age to retire. However, her vivaciousness makes her seem like an ingénue. She graciously invited me to her home. It is in a well-heeled suburb, yet the house appeared to be just a small, unremarkable cottage. When I came in, it was large and full of light; I realized that most of the building was set on a hillside in back and overlooked their back garden.

Barbara's parents were first-generation Jewish Americans; her parents emigrated from Russia. She was an only child, raised in a two-room apartment in New York City; her parents lived there for their entire marriage, and Barbara was with them until she went to college. The family lived hand-to-mouth, so there was never a discussion of financial charity to others. Although their family did not belong to a temple, Barbara felt that it was easy to be Jewish. One did not have to belong to an organized religious group to be part of the neighborhood community, which seemed to have fewer divisions than we commonly see today. It was a cruel surprise to Barbara when, after graduate school, she encountered anti-Semitism when she applied for a teaching job.

After their modest upbringings, Barbara and her husband were concerned about raising their own three children in more affluent circumstances. At one point, during a large storm, the power went out; they lit candles and all slept in the same room. Although the children thought this was exciting and delightful, Barbara knew what it was like to live with deprivation all the time. Because of this, she and her husband worked to transmit their values to the kids. They got them involved at a young age as volunteers, helped them to understand their fortunate level of affluence, and taught that there are obligations that come with comfort. Today the children are adults, and each works in a helping profession; one as a teacher, one as a public health worker, and one with people who are incarcerated.

Today Barbara and her husband are well-off. He is a prominent lawyer who spends a considerable portion of his time doing pro bono work on international reconciliation and reparation cases. Barbara has worked as a volunteer with a professional theater company for the past fourteen years and says she always plays maternal characters. They helped to start a local Jewish community center, and Barbara often hosts large groups for holiday meals at their house. She emphasized that most of the major Jewish holidays are celebrated around a table in a home; some Jewish traditions even speak of having at least ten people attending to say certain prayers. She invites many more people than this, as she wants to make sure no one in her community is alone or without family warmth at holiday times.

---

act on it. For others, it will be a reasonable and carefully thought-out decision based on the facts. For most of us, it is a combination of thoughts and emotions—a powerful mix!

Consumerist Culture

This book primarily assumes an American perspective. In the United States, we are inundated with messages about increasing our happiness through consumption. The whole advertising industry dedicates itself to finding ways to tell us we would be happier, better-looking, healthier, or better-liked if we bought a certain product. Generosity takes a different form in cultures with an alternative understanding about the best use of material resources. Amy-Lee, who had just come back from China at the time of our interview, was struck by the differences in that culture. She said that the legacy of Communism, with an anti-consumerist ideology, has created a generation of people who are unfamiliar with wanting unusual or luxury goods. Now that China is opening up to more public commerce, international brands are trying to educate the Chinese people in what Amy-Lee called "the vocabulary of wanting things." This led her to reflect on American consumerism. She said, "We are taught from an early age to want things, to covet things. So when you get a paycheck, you see the money and immediately think: What do I want? Yet, there is another way to use money. We have to redefine a different use of money for ourselves."

> To receive everything, one must open one's hands and give.
>
> Taisen Deshimaru

The most culturally challenging action in a consumer society may be to give away money to benefit others, with no reciprocation or personal benefit expected in return. American culture emphasizes earning and financial status, spending beyond basic needs, and aspiring to various forms of luxury. It is indeed the American Dream, even if you have to go into unreasonable debt to achieve it. In addition to this *get-and-spend* mentality, media messages fuel fears of economic insecurity, even in "boom" times. We often hear that Social Security will go bankrupt before we retire, or that Medicare will not survive, that real-estate fluctuations will drive us into deeper recession, and always that we have not saved enough to prepare for old age. The American culture is not an easy one in which to be generous.

As you read this book, you may find that you have thoughts fueled by these cultural messages about obtaining comfort, happiness, and security through money. You may want to record these thoughts in your journal to see if they shift as you engage in new experiences. These may include:

- This is fine for people who have lots of spare money, but I need everything I have to get by.
- If I give without bounds, people will take advantage of me. I don't want to be a sucker.
- Giving away money is throwing it away; often it is not used well, so it goes to waste.
- If I lose my hard-won financial standing, I will never get it back.
- When I retire, I want to have plenty of money to support myself. It is the only thing I can rely upon and it will be terrible if I do not have enough.
- I already do what I can; you are just trying to convince me to write big checks!
- The only insurance for the future is to have a lot of savings.
- My modest donations or working in a food kitchen do not solve the problem. Does it really matter what I give?
- The rich DO have a better life.

If you have any of these thoughts, do not dismay—everybody does. Consider them as signals that you are in new territory, not as obstacles to halt your exploration. It has been said that courage is not the absence of fear, but perseverance despite it. When you have thoughts such as these, try to imagine other possibilities. By the time you reach the end of this book, you might have come to a different view. In any case, generosity necessitates being reasonable and optimistic, yet not fearful, about what we need to ensure our own survival. It also requires an openness to others, the ability to be moved and inspired, and to act on those emotions.

Wealth and Poverty

Consumer culture has generated unbounded desires in many people. It also has created a widespread and collective fantasy about wealth. Without it, foolish spending on lotteries and other kinds of gambling might perish. It has had a profound effect on how we think about wealth and poverty. All of our ideas about poverty, wealth, cautiousness with our resources, and generosity were learned. Some of us have had powerful experiences with a family member or mentor who taught us about these concepts and how to live accordingly. We also learn from our own life experiences. Generally speaking, *poor* and *rich* are both determined by a specific context, and their definitions are flexible. In a neighborhood where a lot of underprivileged people live, a family may be considered rich because they have a nice television, yet they are still living with meager resources. Likewise, compared with their neighbors, a middle-class family might feel poor in a high-income area. Clearly, these are subtle and complicated issues. Your own experiences provide a good place to start sorting them out.

When you understand how you came to your beliefs about wealth and poverty, you have taken the first step toward taking a fresh look at them, as an adult. Then you can decide which of these beliefs you want to keep, and which you want to revise. This book aims to help you free yourself from unreasonable fears about poverty and from unrealistic fantasies about wealth.

Your history and experiences will also inform how you understand your current resources and opportunities. For instance, people who grow up with very limited resources may as adults be insecure and overly cautious about their resources—this might be called a "poverty mentality." Yet, someone growing up in the same conditions may exercise incredible open-handedness, perhaps out of an understanding of what it is like to grow up in material poverty. Similarly, someone who grows up with a surplus of resources may orient themselves toward their own comfort and luxury alone, insensitive to the needs of people with lower incomes. Other people from resource-rich families may grow up to be cautious or frugal about spending money on themselves, regardless of whether or not they give their money to others.

> My bounty is as boundless as the sea,
> My love as deep. The more I give to thee,
> The more I have, for both are infinite.
> William Shakespeare,
> Juliet in *Romeo and Juliet*

If you are financially well-off, consider looking in your surrounding community and daily life, to try to have a direct experience with people living in poverty and get a fresh view of what their life is like. In some ways, being without financial resources may be more difficult and intractable than you imagine. You might also be surprised by the great richness, happiness, and love that people living in poverty experience in their lives just as they are. Having some personal experiences might give you a fuller picture of the concerns and joys of underprivileged people, things you have in common, and factors that affect their lives and yours.

If you find yourself strapped for resources, try to look around yourself and have direct experiences with people who have more material wealth than yours. This might be difficult because those communities can be purposefully closed and physically isolated. For the purposes of this research, it will be sufficient to find anyone you consider wealthier than you are and engage them in conversation. If you gain more knowledge about what life is like for someone who is wealthier, it might help you better understand their experience and viewpoint—as opposed to the way tabloids or popular culture depict people with wealth. You may find that you have things in common, and that their lives hold just as many challenges and delights as yours.

As we consider how to be skillful in our generosity, it's useful to employ the concept of *discernment*. Indeed, it is an important part of any practice. It means using keen insight, perception, and judgment and is often used in religious contexts. Generosity takes a fair amount of discernment—how much to give, to whom, in what form, to what end? Giving is not a termination point; it is an opening to the potential for solidarity and kinship. For this reason, discernment is vital to developing clarity of purpose and groundedness in yourself so that your giving is respectful, empowering, and full of love. You might ponder how to inhabit the duality of living within a consumer-driven culture, with its flood of messages, and living outside of it, which you might find more enriching. Finding the proper balance takes trial and error, perceptiveness, and wisdom.

You Are Already Generous

Everyone is generous in her or his own way. Sometimes people are generous only in small or specific instances, but we can also boldly commit to it every day with every resource available. Aren't you already generous? Hasn't there been a time when you cared for someone who was sick, nurtured a young person, or benefited someone without them knowing it? Maybe you do not think of yourself as generous because, like all of us, you are sometimes impatient or do not share what you have when you could, or your idea of what constitutes generosity is too grand to reach. Most people give without a long-range intention or a giving plan to follow—they see someone is in need and if they are able to help them by giving, they do. And when they are asked to give financially to a nonprofit organization doing important work or to their religious community, they do if they can.

Build on what you already do in your own setting and activities. You have probably had experiences when you were generous beyond what was expected and have known the good feelings that come from those actions. You most likely have supported a number of charitable organizations. You have relationships with friends and loved ones who at times call on you to give what you can, and you do. What if you put those things together? What if you made a plan out of those elements so that your generosity was more intentional and ambitious? What if you intend to be generous every day, in as many situations as possible? How might that change the way you experience your life?

As you explore these questions, it will be important to have some solid and fact-based ideas about your current generosity. This includes all types of generosity: volunteer efforts, financial gifts, and even generous acts within your immediate family. As you do this work, you might slip into feeling that you are not good enough, you have not done enough in the past, or your generosity does not measure up to that of others. It may be more straightforward for you to challenge yourself and feel the benefits of generosity if you keep in mind that you are already a generous person and strive to build on that strength.

Start Where You Are

Wherever you are, try to be generous from right there. In some instances, people in the most dire circumstances are still able to give generously to someone else. In other instances, people with many resources give in a challenging way, right to the edge of their available resources. Generosity is based on your intent and willingness to stretch to help others gain what they need.

The practice of generosity is not always easy. It may challenge you. This book intends to help you try to be just a little more generous every day. It affirms how generous you are and encourages you to grow your practice by being more inspired and acting more consciously. You are not being asked to leave your home and give all of your worldly possessions to the poor. If that is what you are called to do, you may need more support than this book can offer. However, most of us can make a significant difference in the world without giving up the things that we deem deeply valuable. And as you read, remember to be generous and loving to yourself. In the end, being generous is an affirmation of hope in the future. It activates hope and provides a reason to hope. You give to someone so that their life improves, and through your gesture of love you may also help to increase their hopefulness.

PRACTICES

The Generosity Assessment

Since you are already a generous person, this chapter includes a Generosity Self-Assessment to help you gauge where you are on this path. This questionnaire helps you look honestly about your current generosity, so please fill it out completely right now, before you read further. If you are uncomfortable writing in the book, make a copy and fill it out. Either way, you will gain the most from writing out the answers and keeping them as a record of your current efforts and what you intend to do today. The assessment has space to capture your thoughts as you go through it. Many people are surprised when they see what they are thinking and doing put together in this way. As you move through this book, you will gain more information about generosity. Later, those initial thoughts may be helpful and interesting to you. You can also take this assessment again to notice any change that happens.

Journaling

Compose a letter as if you were sending it to someone, but write it to your current self from the perspective of you five years in the future. In this letter "from the future," tell what your life is like and how you are living as a more intentionally generous person. What do you do? With whom do you spend time? Who benefits from your generosity and how? What effect is your generosity having?

At the end of your letter, take a few minutes and make notes about how you will know that you reached your vision. What indicators will tell you that you have become the person you had hoped?

Keep the letter in your journal so that you can review it in the future. It may give you a picture of where you have been.

Generosity Self-Assessment

Introduction

This self-reflection is a starting point to prompt your thinking about how you give, when you give, and where you give. It is a tool to assist you in becoming more conscious about your giving practices and patterns; it is not an evaluation or self-improvement manual. Although you will be encouraged to discuss your findings with others, the revelation of any of your personal information will be left to your own judgment.

You may return to this many times in the months and years ahead: The results will undoubtedly shift to reflect changes in your life and resources. Hopefully it will prompt you to see the ways in which you are generous and to help you discover the places where your current generosity practice might be enhanced or deepened.

There is, of course, no right answer, so feel free to circle more than one possible choice. At the end of most sections, you have been provided a place for notes (please use your journal or another sheet of paper as needed). You can use this space to reflect on the questions asked or, alternatively, reflect on thoughts the questions might have triggered for you. You should use it in ways that you find most meaningful.

Self-Care

I take care of my physical, emotional, and spiritual health:
    a. Not enough
    b. Adequately
    c. Exquisitely

How well do I balance my self-care/financial needs and my care for others?

_____

_____

_____

_____

_____

Personal and Professional Engagement

In adult life, I have received assistance from friends, family and/or co-workers:
  a. Regularly and often
  b. Occasionally, when needed
  c. Only when I was desperate for help
  d. It feels like no one ever helps me

I am _____ to help friends, family, and/or coworkers in a time of personal need.
  a. Somewhat likely
  b. Likely
  c. Very likely

I am _____ to assist family and friends in achieving their personal or professional goals.
  a. Somewhat likely
  b. Likely
  c. Very likely

Last year, I asked that friends and family make donations or volunteer to charitable organizations, in lieu of giving me gifts or in other circumstances.
  a. ___ Yes
  b. ___ No

In situations where I am being paid, I tend to:
  a. Offer periodic advice when asked
  b. Mentor one or more staff members on an ongoing basis
  c. Formally and regularly help support people in their professional development

Notes: _____

_____

_____

_____

Appreciation

I tend to notice when people help others and thank them for their contribution.

    a.   Somewhat likely
    b.   Likely
    c.   Very likely

I am _____ to take time to reflect on the good I have done for others, or on the good that I observe others doing.

    a.   Somewhat likely
    b.   Likely
    c.   Very likely

I _____ feel a sense of accomplishment for the volunteer work and financial contribution I make.

    a.   Infrequently
    b.   Frequently
    c.   Always

When receiving appreciation from others, I:

    a.   Become embarrassed
    b.   Try to help them understand how much they have given me as well
    c.   Take it in and cherish it

Financial Assistance

If I were as generous as I would like to be, I would set an annual goal of giving approximately _____ percent of my yearly income.

In the past year, I would estimate that I donated to worthy causes at _____ percent of my adjusted gross income.

Thinking of my financial contributions, I tend to:
- a. Contribute in large amounts at tax time, holidays, or other special occasions
- b. Contribute usually only when asked
- c. Give regularly and frequently
- d. I have difficulty saying no when I am asked for assistance

As an adult, have you ever had to rely on financial assistance from others? __Yes __No

If yes, what was that like for you?
If not, what do you imagine that would be like?

Notes (feel free to list organizations to which you give regularly):

_____

_____

_____

_____

My Time and Care

If I were as generous with my time as I would like to be, how much time per month would I volunteer to benefit others (both in formal roles and informally/spur of the moment)?

_____

Thinking about the past year, I would say on average I volunteered _____ number of hours each month (both formally and informally).

Thinking of my contribution of time and care, I tend to:
    a.   Volunteer large amounts of time around holidays, special events, or campaigns
    b.   Volunteer usually only when asked
    c.   Volunteer regularly and frequently
    d.   I have difficulty saying no when I am asked for assistance

When receiving help from others, I:
    a.   Often feel bad and do not take time to appreciate their efforts
    b.   Appreciate their efforts only if they give the assistance exactly as I need it
    c.   Am grateful for whatever effort they can make

Notes: _____
_____
_____
_____

Further Reflection

What kind of relationship (or lack of relationship) is there between the way I give my gifts of money and the way I give my gifts of time and care? _____
_____
_____
_____

Focus in Giving

When deciding where to donate my money, time, or other resources, I usually:
  a. Respond when people ask or I see an opportunity
  b. Select people or organizations that focus on issues that are important to me
  c. Select people or organizations that are known for accomplishing their mission
  d. Research and select people or organizations that will use my contribution to help as many people in need as possible

I support causes, organizations, or individuals through:
  a. Support of leadership
  b. Donation of time and/or money for specific projects or events that are highly important to me/them
  c. Donation of time and/or money *on a regular basis* to support their work

As a volunteer, I am most likely to directly help others by:
  a. Informally offering help when needed
  b. Holding a committed financial and/or volunteer position
  c. Doing indirect work to change systems

When volunteering time and care, I tend to take:
  a. A leadership role
  b. A supportive role

When contributing financially, I tend to take:
  a. A leadership role
  b. A supportive role

Notes: _____

_____

_____

_____

Reflections on This Generosity Self-Assessment

Spend some time looking at how you answered these questions and the notes you may have written. Did you notice ways in which you are currently generous that you don't typically think about? Did you find any patterns in the way you give of your time and care and your financial giving? Are your giving patterns spiritually fulfilling and meaningfully connecting you with others? Are there ways that your giving patterns aren't working for you as well as you would like? What emotions came up for you as you did this survey?

_____

_____

_____

_____

_____

_____

_____

_____

_____

_____

_____

CHAPTER 2

The Generous Receiver

Although giving cannot exist without someone or something to receive the gift, the role of the receiver in these transactions often goes unrecognized. The recipient's response can either increase or blunt the confidence and motivation of the giver. We can encourage generosity in others by cultivating our ability to receive graciously. When people become more gracious at receiving, it opens up their generosity in new ways. You cannot be a truly generous giver without also being a generous receiver.

We all know how wonderful it is to receive a gift or a gesture that fills us with delight. I remember how I looked forward to my birthday as a child. Back then, I focused on whatever toy or game I craved that particular year. With age, non-material gifts, such as a caring touch or handwritten note, have come to matter more to me. Also, I focus on accepting the intention of the giver. That someone knows enough about me and cares enough to give me just the right gift touches me deeply. To support this process, and to develop myself as a generous receiver, I have tried to be open and available—knowable to the people around me—so they can more accurately assess what I need or want.

When a gift is given to you skillfully, it carries a special recognition of you as the recipient—what you like, what has meaning for you, what might touch you. Or it can be an action or offering that responds to an urgent need the giver sees. Giving and receiving operate on a number of levels at once. Whatever action or object being offered, it carries with it an intention, and it creates a connection or disconnection. Perhaps the most basic form of generosity is allowing someone to be present with you—to witness you in your grief, hear you in your questioning, or join with you in celebration. If you are willing, you can grow your ability to be a skillful receiver and increase your joy when even modest things are offered to you. A first step in growing your receiving skill is to become more aware of things you might otherwise take for granted.

Liz (p. 174) has had unusual experiences in receiving. These experiences have given her an outsider's perspective on some things that one might normally take for granted. For instance, at a party in Bosnia, a Bosnian she was dating said, "When your friends get drunk, they are very happy, and my friends get sad." At the party, while people seemed to get more and more morose, Liz realized that almost everyone there had been in a concentration camp. These Bosnians carried emotional scars from violent experiences that Liz did not have—the absence of which allowed her to have greater natural joy in life. Upon returning to the United States, Liz was struck by this contrast on a beautiful spring day in Boston, where people were socializing and studying in Harvard Yard. As she looked at them, she wondered if they had any sense of the simple gift of peace in their community that benefited them all the time.

> Receiving is an art. . . . So many people have been deeply hurt because their gifts were not well received.
> Let us be good receivers.
> Henri J.M. Nouwen

We are certainly aware of areas and instances in our own communities that are not like Harvard Yard on that spring day—which may be unsafe or seriously degraded economically. Yet, when you are given the opportunity to see your culture from an outsider's view, you might be more grateful for many aspects of your life that you might otherwise take for granted.

While living in a war zone, or even being helpless and needing regular personal care in our own community, may seem a distant and extreme possibility, people are generous to us all the time. We work under the illusion that we are fully independent operators. Yet we depend on thousands, maybe hundreds of thousands, of unseen people in multiple systems to support everything we do— for our food, transportation, governance, safety, education, energy, communications, and many other aspects of our lives. Whenever we make a mistake, there is usually someone who acts generously to help us correct it or compensate for it in some way.

Most of us, as children, learned lessons about receiving: *Always say "thank you." It is the thought that counts. Act grateful, even when the gift is not wanted. Write a thank you note.* Good manners acculturate our children to get along well with others. Although they are a basic concept, they require us to master our feelings. For instance, when we receive an unwanted gift, we still respond graciously. In this way, manners help us to be sensitive to the feelings of others, and so they provide a training ground and a platform for true acts of generosity.

Challenges to Receiving

When manners are memorized and deployed mechanically, they inhibit the possibility of connection rather than opening it up. Manners can be used as a defense against vulnerability, even to a potentially loving gesture.

Giving and receiving inhabit two sides of the same coin; one does not exist without the other. We cannot be a world full of givers if there is no one to accept our gifts. Yet many people, especially generous people, find giving to be a wonderful experience and receiving to be uncomfortable, embarrassing, or even shameful. You may endure receiving, out of need or politeness, thinking that you are not revealing the fact that it makes you uncomfortable. Yet if you are absorbed in your own response in those moments, then you are not fully present to the person who is giving to you. They will notice that you're not fully attentive; people are sensitive to these cues. If you believe that "it is the thought that counts," then you have just cut off their thought by engaging in your inter-

text continues on page 28

JIM AND RITA

The more I give, the more I am able to give; it is just easier to do.

—Rita

In middle age, Jim and Rita are a close married couple and, in fact, seem much alike. They are of similar compact size and obviously relish engagement and conversation, which gives an impression of youthfulness. We met over lunch in a sandwich shop that was a little too busy and loud, yet both Rita and Jim kept their focus on our conversation and never seemed distracted. Jim is a minister in an urban church; beyond his friendliness, he seems reflective and considered. Their children are now grown and living elsewhere. Although Rita has always been a professional woman and has no official function in the congregation, she clearly dedicates her time volunteering there. The church is right in the city center, yet one gets the impression that their congregation is fairly small and has a family-like culture. It is also obvious that there is real concern about low-income families living near the church, which are served with direct service programs by church members. Rita and Jim come across as examples of people who give their lives and their resources in service to others, expecting nothing in return, yet feel fulfilled.

Both Rita and Jim grew up in relatively low-income families where they lived paycheck-to-paycheck; nevertheless, they were always encouraged to volunteer and be charitable. Both have had their church as a central part of their lives since childhood. Jim grew up in a household where financial giving was practiced even in early childhood; he had to earn his own allowance by doing chores and then was required to dedicate part of it to the church's collection plate. Rita also was taught to give early in life, with both money and time. Her family stories about giving are full of charming

26

anecdotes, like her father driving 200 miles out of his way to bring a hitchhiking active duty soldier home.

They met when they were younger and living in a small semi-rural community in the middle of the United States. There, they were involved in growing theater and other arts ventures as entrepreneurs—I got the sense they "teamed up" to help make shared projects successful. One of these was an arts festival they started, which became the largest in the state and is still going on today.

After they had two young children, Jim was hospitalized with a serious illness. Later, Jim decided to go to seminary, which put the family under considerable financial strain. Although Jim and Rita did their best to be self-sufficient, people from their community found ways to assist with their children and support in other ways. They also had an acquaintance who acted as an "angel" and would occasionally send them money, just when they needed it most.

The transition from arts producer to minister seems natural for Jim, partly due to his personality, which is engaged yet thoughtful, and partly because there are similarities between running an arts organization and a church. Although Rita and Jim clearly do not have a lot of extra money, they are generous with the money they have. Yet, their stories are of deep personal connection and spiritual growth through giving and receiving.

---

nal challenge rather than appreciating their intention. Being a good receiver requires balancing authenticity with concern for the responses of others.

What makes it so much harder to receive than to give? Many of us associate needing something from someone else with shame or a lack of self-sufficiency. This was true for Anthony, (p. 90) who worked hard to balance his own giving and receiving. He said, "I realized that the receiving side of generosity was a real edge for me because it made me feel like a failure." In some cases, it is a matter of poor self-esteem; people believe they do not deserve the assistance or gift. In that case, the more the gift is wanted, the less deserved it may feel and the harder to receive. Other people feel that accepting support or a gift is inconvenient for the person giving it and they do not want be a burden, even to those who care about them most.

As generous people, we need to keep in mind that giving can be potent, powerful stuff. In giving we can elevate the recipients— make them more self-sufficient and feel good about themselves—or we can put them down so that they feel dependent and insufficient. And when we receive we accept a vulnerable position, subject to the inclination of the giver—we can either be treated poorly or supported with caring. Part of being a more skillful recipient is learning to a) understand ourselves as naturally and unavoidably having needs, b) graciously accepting what people can and want to give, while c) retaining our own sense of efficacy and value.

Because Anthony earned more than his partner, he was comfortable bearing more of their shared expenses. Later, Anthony's partner got a new, higher-paying job and Anthony lost his; the arrangement was completely reversed. This made Anthony uncomfortable. Since money can symbolize self-reliance, financial factors like these can have a powerful effect.

Anthony's story illustrates that accepting money from others is especially fraught in our culture. Yet as a generous receiver, one might accept a monetary gift as a blessing and see how financial generosity can help to forge relationships. Rita and Jim (p. 26) tell of an "angel" they had in their lives while Jim was in seminary. This was a man they knew who every so often would send them a check. Rita said he always seemed to know just when they were about to have financial trouble—when their car broke down out of the blue or their washer needed repair. This friend never expected anything in return, but he gave to them because he supported their goal of going into religious service, and he knew they were short on resources. Without much personal contact with him, Jim and Rita developed a strong and enduring bond with their "angel."

Independence

American culture is built on the idea of independence. One of our country's founding documents even uses the word: *The Declaration of Independence!* Regardless of circumstance, creed, class, ethnicity, race, or ability, fully grown adults are supposed to be able to take care of themselves. This idea imbues all aspects of our culture: our literature (such as the Horatio Alger "rags to riches" stories), our political system (which allows for party affiliation as well as "independent" voters), our cultural myths (the American Dream celebrates financial independence), and even our language (with expressions such as *to stand on your own two feet* or *to pull yourself up by your bootstraps*). Whether you were brought up to feel assured that you will have enough and others will help you if you need it, or that you can never fully trust in sufficiency and support, you probably place highly value in being independent.

Despite her positive experiences in other parts of the world, which have shifted her understanding of giving and receiving, Liz sums up the ethic beautifully: "Receiving is very difficult. I'm American, so I am self-reliant. I don't want to too often rely on other people."

However, your independence must be flexible enough so that you can still connect deeply with others, and can rely on them when you need to. Rita and Jim recalled a time when their two children were toddlers and Rita worked full-time as the bread-winner. At this point, Jim was hospitalized with a serious illness for almost a month. Their friends asked Rita how they could help, but she always told them she was "fine." One particular friend from church offered to take care of the children so Rita could go to the hospital and spend some time alone with Jim. Although Rita demurred, this friend followed her to the hospital anyway and whisked the kids away for a while. Rita said, "I broke down in tears because it was just what I needed." In this instance, Rita's idea about needing to be independent almost prevented her from getting the help she needed, and from allowing her church friend to be of service.

Being parented is a wonderful model for receiving. We are all born in weakness and must rely on others, usually our parents, to attend our every need. We would not survive without this care; our only role is to be a receiver and to grow. These basic needs decrease as we grow and develop, eventually allowing an increase in our independence. But during times of crisis and at the end of our lives, most of us will again become vulnerable and rely on the loving care of others. A family member, someone we know as a friend, or a member of our community may care for us. But it might also be someone we did not know before, such as a medical professional or a Good Samaritan. How we accept their care may determine what that experience is like for us, as well as for the people providing the care. Gracefully accepting care may also determine the quality of that care; the people who appreciate and welcome such generosity tend to receive better treatment.

Daniel (p. 70) is aware of this and has started to prepare himself. He said, "If I live that long, it will be a challenge to receive care. I have to think about it now and do some soul-searching to get control of some of my impulses and urges. At some point, you have to let go and accept people's assistance."

Some say that we are always vulnerable, that our independence is an illusion, and that we survive only as the beneficiaries of people who paved the way before us—our forebears; our communities; a higher power, creator, God, or whatever we believe. When we recognize that, sooner or later, we all will rely upon the generosity of others—and in fact have unfulfilled needs most of the time—we will develop empathy and build solidarity with people or issues we hope to benefit with our giving. We are joined in a common neediness, even if the specific necessities differ.

When our self-perception is tied to taking care of ourselves with no help from others, we experience fewer opportunities for accepting the normal give-and-take of care in relationships. This level of independence can lead to an unreasonable and rigid standard of self-reliance. If this approach endures, then our lack of experience with receiving might even make it difficult to assess whether we need someone else's care; our understanding of the dynamic of giving and receiving atrophies from disuse. Those of us who are seniors, for example, may not adjust our concept of independence as we age, making us unable to adapt to a need for more assistance.

> Giving connects two people, the giver and the receiver, and this connection gives birth to a new sense of belonging.
> Deepak Chopra

Anthony told me this story about his education in receiving. He was part of the hospice care team when a friend's wife was dying of cancer. She refused to adjust her need to be in control and self-sufficient, which made it harder for those who wanted to love and take care of her. Anthony learned that he did not want to do that: "I want to be gracious at receiving care."

Being a good receiver requires balancing our personal authenticity with concern for our response to the giver. Sometimes, people will try to give to you something out of the generosity of their hearts, yet it is not what you need or want. You will have to decide what is the most generous action in that moment. It may be to accept the gift as graciously as you can, recognizing that this person is reaching out to you and what they give is of secondary importance. Or it may be that you will open up your heart to that person and let them know what you really need, so they can give more appropriate gifts. This can do much to grow a connection and relationship. Your most generous focus could be to honor that person for their effort, thoughtfulness, care, and actions. If you have that spirit, then you have accepted their true gift and have given them a sense of belonging and success.

Being Genuine, Being Present

Sometimes a gift-giver expects reciprocation. Most of us usually expect an expression of gratitude, even if it is just a thank you. There is a remarkable difference between a rote thank you, especially if that response masks awkwardness, and an authentic thank you. This is a qualitative difference; it does not mean speaking loudly or jumping up and down. The deeply appreciative recipient conveys this feeling through tone of voice, expression, and demeanor. If the gift or support comes from a distance, we can convey warmth and sincerity through other forms of communication as well, such as a note, email, or phone call.

Jim told me a wonderful and simple example of this learning. Before he was in ministry, he worked as a theater director. When friends would see him, they would often mention seeing his plays. One Sunday, a woman he knew came up to him at church and said, "I came to the show last night and it was brilliant." Jim had attended the show the night before as well and found it disappointing compared with other performances. His response to her was, "Well I wish you had seen a better show . . ." The woman stopped Jim mid-sentence and said, "Jim, when someone gives you a compliment, say thank you and shut up." That lesson awakened Jim to how his lack of presence for receiving a gift could offend the giver.

To be generous when receiving, you must really be present in the moment and set aside any awkwardness, embarrassment, or feeling of entitlement. The giver has gone out of their way to give you something, whether it is a chocolate chip cookie, assistance with a household-repair job, or significant financial resources. You are expected to be grateful, and you probably are. Being fully present when you receive something will open the way for a reaction from you that will gratify the person giving you the gift.

The next time someone gives you a gift, try pausing for a moment. Accept the gift with as much presence as you have. Without being dramatic, take a slow, deep breath before saying anything. Then say thank you, and think of your expression of thanks as a separate gift, a new gift—related to the gift that you were just given but separate, honoring the person who faces you.

At times, you might sense an imbalance between what is given and what is received. For instance, someone might give a modest amount, but it is just what is needed by the recipient and allows them to make major changes in their life. At other times, a large financial amount can be given, and the benefit is not obvious or seems modest. But true generosity is seldom wasted. Even if it appears to have made no difference, the sheer act of honoring the people involved and adding just a bit to the project can mean it will move forward and eventually be successful.

Receiving precedes giving, whether in the realm of our personal history as a defenseless baby; our cultural history, as many before us created the context in which we live; our scientific history, as our brain capacity evolved from less intelligent primates; or our religious beliefs, as some people believe God is the originator of all gifts. When we become more conscious about, practiced in, and intentional in our receiving, our generosity will bloom. A simple gift can spawn a new enterprise, an improved self-concept, or a close relationship. The possibilities are endless. To take advantage of them, we must be generous receivers.

PRACTICES

Noticing Yourself as a Receiver

As you go about your daily life, notice yourself when someone gives you something. Consider large and small gifts (including compliments and information). How does each gift make you feel inside? What is your most common reaction when receiving? What factors prompt a different reaction as a receiver?

Gift Inventory

Each person has unique qualities and attributes. We can consider that at least some of these have been received from our parents and ancestors; from God (depending on our belief system); or through the guidance of our relatives, teachers, and supervisors. That is why they are gifts. Here is an activity to help you clarify your gifts:

Take a piece of blank piece of paper and prepare to brainstorm in response to the question below. Write down whatever pops in your head. Do not edit or judge before you get it on the paper. Write until your brainstorming is complete, then edit and put your list in order of importance. It will be useful to you later in this book (and perhaps for a long time!).

What gifts have you received and created that you can offer the world?

Journaling

Spend some time with your journal and tell the following stories:

1. Write about a time when someone was generous to you. Start with the most powerful story you remember, and then feel free to add others. For each story, write down what you learned from the experience.
2. Write about a time when you were generous to someone else. Start with the most powerful story you remember, and then feel free to add others. Make an effort to suspend your modesty and be frank about what you did. For each story, write down what you learned from the experience.

CHAPTER 3

Learning Generosity and Guiding Others

How does someone learn to be generous? What helped them step out of the get-and-spend cycle to be more altruistic? The people interviewed for this book told stories from early in their lives about family members, friends, and communities who gave generously. As you read these stories, notice whether they conjure up thoughts of your own history. Your memories may help you understand how the arc of your life has either supported your development as a giving person or created challenges you have had to overcome. This self-awareness can make you more clear-sighted and responsive as you move toward more skillful giving. And because all these people are intentionally generous, they shed light on effective ways to help people grow their generosity.

Not all of the interviewees' childhood stories involved money; some were related to giving time, caring, or effort, or just being present with others. Most parents do not engage with their children about the family finances until they are old enough to have an allowance, and even then only in the simplest way. It takes time to learn how money works. However, even a young child might notice the effects of financial hardship or affluence on their family, especially as compared with others they know. And younger children may also understand the effort their mother takes sitting with someone who is grieving, or the sacrifices that the whole family makes by inviting a non-relative to live with them. Non-monetary generosity is a good basis on which to start understanding altruism, which can later develop into financial giving.

Some interviewees were taught about giving money directly, either through explicit examples of their parents, by being required to make charitable donations from their allowance, or by being told to refuse money for volunteer work. This helped those with more affluent backgrounds to understand how they might use their resources to benefit others. People with limited resources might have learned that one can always spare a bit to share with others who need it. And although the people I interviewed said their parents were generous people, aside from some religious giving, those who knew about their parents' charitable behavior were exceptional.

In stories from their adult lives, almost every person interviewed told of times or experiences when they came to some point of change, a tipping point, where they shifted in their understanding—that their own resources might be used as tools to connect to and benefit others. You may have experienced this kind of epiphany yourself. Others spoke of mentors who modeled the benefits of being financially generous, or they engaged with a community that helped teach them about financial giving. This two-stage process of learning in childhood and developing in adulthood is useful when thinking about how we might impart generosity to both kids and adults. The interviews revealed five ways to provide a good grounding in generosity. All of these strategies are made more effective by our being more forthcoming about our own financial giving and volunteering.

- We can give children direct guidance and model generous behavior. This may or may not include financial generosity.
- We can expose children and adults to people who are disadvantaged or need support.
- We can invite others to participate in meaningful volunteering or related donorship.

- Those of us who are more practiced in generosity can make ourselves available as mentors, and cultivate guiding relationships with those who are less experienced.
- Finally, we can create and invite people to join a community of practice where people find kinship in the development and practice of generosity.

Some people think that talking openly about personal giving comes across as arrogant. Good practice does not involve trumpeting one's good deeds or listing an impressive amount of a donation. No one interviewed spoke in this egotistical way. Yet, they all spoke at length and in inspiring ways about their giving. They told about how they came to their desire to be generous, what their experiences have been, what these steps on the path of generosity have meant for them, and what they hope for in the future. These are unique personal histories; some may be similar to yours, yet all of them led to people who had developed their own generosity.

Instruction and Modeling in a Family of Origin

Studies of financial giving trends in multiple generations have shown that the giving of parents or guardians correlates strongly with the giving of their children when they become adults. This is true of both giving that goes to nonprofits and religious giving.[6] In fact, the parent or guardian's behavior in religious giving has some effect on their adult children's giving to nonprofits as well.

Let's start by considering generosity through the interviewees' stories about their family members. Although each person's biography is distinct, you may find that elements of these stories have similarities to your own upbringing. If you notice ways that you learned about being generous in ways aside from those contained in these stories, take note of them as others may benefit from your stories or examples.

As Anthony (p. 90) was growing up, his family opened their house to their community. Even when times were financially rough for the family, they always had surplus food so they could help feed people who needed it. Their home became a destination. So many people came by to talk about their problems, the family used to joke that Anthony's mother ran the neighborhood counseling center. It was only when Anthony got older that he realized the huge commitment his mother made to being that open and available. It made a deep impression on Anthony, and set a pattern for his future behavior.

Rita's (p. 26) father had a reputation for going to extremes to help someone out—especially military veterans. She remembers him building a series of birdfeeders to surround the local Veteran's Administration retirement facility. He kept these continuously stocked with feed to attract birds, since he knew many of the people inside were bedridden and would

> Generosity is giving more than you can, and pride is taking less than you need.
>
> Kahlil Gibran

gain joy in looking out to see them. In another family story, her father picked up a service man hitchhiking and took him two hundred miles out of his way to get him to where he needed to go. The delight and humor with which Rita told these stories shows both love for her father and how important that example was for her.

In some instances, people are taught directly about being charitable. When Henry (p. 136) was a boy, and long before he focused on giving to create change through political influence, he helped his father mow the lawns and shovel the walks for all the elderly people in the neighborhood. His father would say, "Just do it. Don't ask them for money. If they give you a tip, that is fine, but just do it." And although Henry's father ran a local restaurant, where the whole family worked almost every day of the year, his father always volunteered and gave small amounts to many different organizations.

Although Brad (p. 164) was raised in a wealthy family, he is old enough to remember how hard-hit his family was by the Great Depression. His father lost his job and was out of work with no income for a period of time. Yet no matter hard it was for them, the family still contributed to their church community; he remembers putting money in the collection plate.

Jim (p. 26) provides an example of someone who was taught explicitly and by example to be generous with all of his resources. Although his family lived from paycheck to paycheck, it was understood in his family that if you had any kind of income, you made charitable gifts. As a child he would help mow his grandfather's lawn and earn fifty cents doing it. Jim's family tithed (giving 10 percent of income to the church), so when he came home with his fifty cents, his family made sure he put a nickel into the Sunday school plate. Jim also recalled that there were always people they did not know well living at their house when he was young. The woman he thinks of as his older sister is actually his cousin, whom the family took in when she needed a place to live.

Tom (p. 40) had perhaps the most direct instruction in giving. His family was openly financially charitable—they made it part of their careers and modeled it for their children. Tom's parents were in the Navy during World War II, and afterward continued with community service throughout their lives. His father was involved in an early form of "corporate responsibility," although that term had not been coined at the time. Corporate responsibility means his company had projects to further social good, beyond the profit motive of the firm or requirements of the law. Tom's father also headed up the local United Way campaign of a large urban region. In addition, their family maintained consistent involvement at their church, where Tom's father was an officer. Tom said, "Their charitable activities were a constant source of discussion in our home." Later, Tom, rather than using his education in elite schools to go into a more lucrative profession, chose to go into the nonprofit sector.

Barbara, (p. 6) who helped found a community center, learned about being generous while growing up amid a lack of resources in New York City. Although she said she learned about caring for
text continues on page 42

39

TOM

*I have seen the transformative effect on people
who give their time and money to good causes.*

—Tom

Tom gave the impression that his life flowed together in one unusually seamless fabric. His social network stretched over his family, his peers, friends, his business partners, his staff, and his volunteers. His values seemed so consistent and his life such a direct expression of them that, listening to him, it was difficult to tease out one thread from another. Tom's charitable giving, his professional service, care for his family, his volunteer service and mentoring, all seem to be part of the same effort; he is marvelously undivided. Mahatma Gandhi said, "You must be the change you want to see in the world." Tom is doing that. We met at a quiet café near his house for the interview, and I came away feeling energized and optimistic. Not only did he make me comfortable, I felt emboldened after our time together. He is a gifted and natural leader.

Tom's history illuminates something about how this consistency may have come about. His parents were both in the Navy during the Second World War and continued with community service throughout their lives. After the war, his mother became involved in local community causes. In addition, their family was involved consistently at their church, where Tom's father was an officer. His father worked for a large corporation and started a program that we might call "corporate responsibility" today. It connected the corporation to charitable causes, which was unheard of at that time. His father was also a leader in United Way for the whole region. Although their family was affluent, his parents set an example of using their time and talents in charitable ways.

Tom went to a prep school and then to an elite college, both of which were near where he grew up. After college, he intended to go to law school and then perhaps join the Foreign Service, but instead he joined the Peace Corps. After his volunteer service, he scrapped his previous plans and stayed with the Peace Corps as an employee. Tom was quickly promoted into leadership and calls his Peace Corps experience "formative." It prepared him to play senior organizational roles in subsequent jobs—all benefiting less privileged people in developing countries.

This led to his first relationship with a mentor, an older man who shared his resources, intelligence, and contacts. Tom has benefited from a number of mentors since then and was now dedicating a significant amount of his time to mentoring younger people.

At the time of our interview, Tom was supporting a couple of kids in college, yet was still able to give a few large gifts to carefully chosen charitable organizations, where he was very familiar with the activities and people involved. These were all related to his own work as a leader in an international nonprofit that supports young adult volunteer efforts.

---

other people from her mother, her family lived "hand-to-mouth." There was never a discussion of financial giving to others. Her family could only afford a small apartment, which they divided by hanging cloth from the ceiling, and her father often worked all night and slept during the day. They could not have guests or host gatherings—there was nowhere to sit and the apartment often needed to be quiet so her father could sleep. Now, as an adult, Barbara gives her time as a volunteer, gives financially, and gives her hospitality—inviting distressed young people to live with her temporarily, holding gatherings for people who might be alone on holidays, and hosting fundraising events.

Mentors, Tipping Points, and Exposure to Need

After childhood, some people build on their learning about giving through close relationships with mentors, usually older people who are not related by blood. When Henry was in college, he had a "surrogate mom" who created change through affecting political discussions. He met her at an anti-war rally and they became close, lifelong friends. Through her example and mentoring, she taught Henry about how financial giving, volunteering, and hosting events could powerfully influence social change conversations. When hosting these events, she included a broad range of people, like Henry, who were not part of the normal circle of influential people.

Author and activist Parker J. Palmer said this about mentoring generosity:

> I think the biggest block to finding generosity of spirit in one's own life is never to have had it modeled for you, so you don't even know what it looks like and you've never known anybody whose own life is animated by that movement of the heart. I think once you've known somebody like that, it's a little harder to not be thinking on it, to not be touched by it, and to not realize how fulfilling it is for one's life. With generosity of spirit I experience a largeness of self;

it doesn't matter whether or not I get something back from it. It is its own reward.[7]

Although Tom grew up in a good environment for developing financial generosity, he also benefited from being engaged by mentors later in life. After he left the Peace Corps, he stayed in South America to work for another international development agency. While there, he was befriended by a local industrialist. This older man made many of his resources available to Tom, introduced him to people, and helped him do his job well. When Tom was a young nonprofit leader back in the United States, he discovered how lonely and unsupported it can feel when you are in charge of an organization. An accomplished older man with no children treated Tom as his son, meeting with him regularly to advise him on all aspects of his work. These experiences helped motivate Tom not only to run a charitable organization, but to actively mentor people who were a generation younger than him, teaching them what he had learned about generosity.

Daniel (p. 70), who became an active financial donor and a full-time volunteer, credits his wife with educating him in the practice of giving; they worked as a team in their efforts. This started with giving to their church, then led to volunteer work in the areas of social justice and support for disabled people before his work life crowded out that time.

Later in his career, Daniel became too busy and stressed at work to do any volunteering, but his life was changed through an act of caring for a near-stranger. On weekends, he would go out in the early morning with his son to their favorite coffee shop for breakfast. There, they met another regular customer, Michael. At one point, Daniel realized that he had not seen Michael in a while, so asked one of the employees where he was. He was told that Michael had been in an accident, resulting in a complex fracture of his leg. Daniel was able to locate Michael and one morning, instead of the coffee shop, he and his son went to the hospital to visit him. Michael had no close relatives or friends, aside from those at the coffee shop. He was being discharged from the hospital in a wheel-chair in three weeks' time. Michael's apartment had steps leading up to it, with no ramp or elevator, so he was anxious about how he would manage. By chance, Daniel happened to own a rarely used portable wheelchair ramp.

Daniel and his son took on Michael's care as a project. First, they installed the ramp at his house, then they set a schedule with Michael to take him out for groceries and do errands, and even advocated with his landlord to create more handicapped accessibility in the building. After about three months, Daniel realized that he had "crossed a threshold"—he really looked forward to his time helping Michael. The project had brought purpose and richness to his relationship with his son, and he had gained a true friend in Michael. The project was the beginning of the reorientation of Daniel's life.

> One isn't necessarily born with courage, but one is born with potential. Without courage, we cannot practice any other virtue with consistency. We can't be kind, true, merciful, generous, or honest.
>
> Maya Angelou

The shifting point for Jim came early in his adulthood, when he was traveling in rural Eastern Europe, not long after the region emerged from the time of scarcity related to the Communist economy. Having been raised in the relative comforts of the United States, Jim was struck by how little these people had, yet how giving they were with their hospitality and, indeed, everything they had. This helped him realize that generosity does not depend on how much you have, but on how much you are willing to share.

Elise and Barry (p. 56) said everything changed in their giving behavior when they adopted their son. Yet Elise also told a story that clearly created another shift for her. She was volunteering for a soup kitchen. In this program, the volunteers brought food out to the recipients, as in a restaurant. Initially, Elise was frightened even to go into the dining room. The first night she was serving, a woman pulled on her sleeve and said, "My feet are really cold and wet." Thinking about what a particularly generous friend might do, Elise took off her own socks. She bent down and put them on the woman, then put the woman's shoes back on and tied them up. The woman was thrilled; the socks were warm because Elise had been wearing them. This was a shifting point for Elise. She said, "That was one of those moments for me; it was so little to give to someone, and it made a big difference to her. I think that people think generosity is just about money, and it's not. It's so much more."

Because Liz (p. 174) constantly moved around the globe during her childhood, her family was more concerned with finding their way around new communities than with making deep connections. For that reason, charitable giving and volunteering were secondary considerations and seldom discussed. However, Liz's parents did convey how important it is to stop what you are doing and provide help when it is needed; they were very generous in this regard. Liz's travels also exposed her to a different perspective on history than many American-educated children. She recalled visiting a castle dungeon in Europe, where she saw descriptions and images of people being flayed and knew that was barbaric. In another instance, a language teacher showed her class a European film about the Hiroshima bombing from a more global perspective than she probably would have gotten in an American school—Liz was horrified. The teacher encouraged her not just to be angry, but to write about it. This helped Liz understand the connection between thoughts and feelings and taking action in the public sphere.

As an adult, possibly the best learning environment for generosity is a community where everyone shares similar values, develops in generosity together, and exercises their giving collectively. Amy-Lee (p. 108) was doing extensive financial planning and considering her giving to her own community when she was interviewed. In her church community, she had heard messages about aligning her financial resources with her values, which caused her to reflect. She was able to observe many people, some of whom gave her personal examples of financial generosity. Through the congregation's community service programs, she was exposed to people in need, and was able to join them and other community members to make a difference in their lives. Amy-Lee saw this project of financial and gift planning as part of a process of maturing and taking her place in the community as a full adult.

Unitarian Universalist and Methodist minister Rebecca Ann Parker tells a wonderful story of this learning evolution in her book *Blessing the World*. While she was serving a United Methodist congregation, during their annual giving drive, a congregant spoke about why he tithes. He said,

> I first began to tithe because I was taught to do so by my church, and my church taught me to obey its teachings. . . . I continued to tithe, however, because . . . the people I most loved and admired tithed: my parents and leaders of the religious community whose lives really challenged me by their goodness. . . . But as my faith matured further, I came to my own reason for tithing . . . because to tithe is to tell the truth about who I am. . . . I am a person who has something to give. I am a person who has received abundantly from life. I am a person whose presence matters in the world, and I am a person whose life has meaning because I am connected to and care about many things larger than myself. If I did not tithe, I would lose track of these truths about who I am.

This man moved from responding to direct instruction, to imitating the example of people he admired, to understanding his giving as an expression of his identity and his relationship to the world. Consider your own unique development; think about people and experiences that instructed or informed you and may have led to a shift in your thinking and actions. These stories may also inform how you might continue on this path or how people you know might still play an active role. The Journaling task at the end of this chapter may help you consider this in more depth.

Guiding the Next Generation and Others

The interviewees' stories shed some light on how we might develop the next generation's generosity. Barbara had been concerned that her children, who had had a more financially comfortable upbringing than she, might not develop into generous adults. She said, with gratitude and pride, that both of her children are now working in helping professions.

Barbara gave an example of what she does to pass her giving practices on to the next generation. In her neighborhood, there is a breakfast restaurant owned by a couple who are Jewish like Barbara. On Christmas each year, the couple closes the restaurant and invites everyone in the community who is financially challenged to come for breakfast. Barbara and her husband volunteer at the event, serving food. She said many of the people who serve there come with their children, both young and old. The beneficiaries are so appreciative, and the other volunteers and children have so much camaraderie that this Christmas event has become a holiday celebration for her as well: "I don't think there is a better feeling than doing something good for someone else."

Daniel actively passes on his experience and knowledge about giving to his children. His story of involving his son in Michael's care is only one example. He and his wife also consciously model behavior for their children and engage them in volunteering in age-appropriate ways. Regarding financial generosity, they do more than teach their children to give from a portion of their allowance; they help them identify where they want to give the money, and in what way they want to deliver their gifts.

According to research, the most effective way a parent can talk to their children about charitable giving is by what is called "other-oriented induction."[8] This involves providing children reasons for giving that focus on the state of the person they hope to help, and how the help will be beneficial.

One way to cultivate generous tendencies in children is to create a cooperative philanthropic venture designed to engage family members of all ages. Ideally, this project would supply opportunities for using all the approaches mentioned in this chapter: direct instruction, modeling behavior, exposure to the people or situations that need support, experiential learning through volunteering, and mentoring.

A final note about learning to be generous: Familial conflicts over inheritances are universal and happen in every era of history. Unfortunately, leaving an inheritance is often the only kind of teaching people offer their survivors regarding their ideas and wishes for their money and possessions. In a time when surviving family members are already in a heightened emotional state, it's no wonder that disagreements over inheritance often lead to conflict and even legal action.

> Almost everyone—regardless of income, available time, age and skills—can do something useful for others and, in the process, strengthen the fabric of our shared humanity.
>
> Bill Clinton

Although there is nothing wrong with leaving a legacy gift to your relatives, it's an ineffective way to teach values or practices for giving. Most people do not leave a legacy to surviving relatives intending to create conflict. To avoid doing so, we should actively impart our ideas and habits about giving to our loved ones throughout our lives and share our specific intentions for our legacy with them while it is still possible to have fruitful discussions. In the process, we might take a more active role in encouraging generous giving and receiving in our family.

PRACTICES

Personal Mission Statement
Organizations create mission statements to clarify and focus their strategies and direction. You can do the same to bring order and prioritization to your own giving. Here are some steps to create a mission statement:

- Start by generating a list of things you care and feel passionate about. These could be causes or problems such as hunger, homelessness, a specific disease, a particular demographic (such as teen girls or the elderly), an issue of public policy (such as prison or health care reform), or patronage of the arts or education. Prioritize the list, with your most passionate at the top.
- In chapter 2, you made a list of the unique gifts that you offer the world. Bring that list back out.
- With your passion and gift lists in front of you, create a mission statement for yourself. Write as much as you want and refine it using these guidelines:
    - Keep it brief, clear, and simple. It should be no more than three or four sentences.
    - It should say what you want to do and become.
    - Keep to positive words and concepts. Look for the words *don't*, *won't*, *not*, *stop*, and *less* and change them to their positive counterparts: *do*, *will*, *start*, *more*.
    - Include a timeline, whether general or specific. Is this a whole-life mission? Is it for the next ten years, or for the coming year?
- Now you have a focus for your generosity. Write or type out a clean copy, and keep it where you can see it regularly.

Journaling

Consider how you were taught and supported in developing your generosity. This might have been in your childhood, youth, or any age. Think about people among your family, friends, friends' families, or neighbors. Also, consider how people you know through your profession, mentoring programs, or volunteer work contributed to your development. This may even include someone you have never met, but who has informed and inspired you.

Make a short list of one to four people who have influenced you in some way about generosity. Note which of these approaches they used to make a difference in you:

- giving guidance
- modeling behavior
- exposing you to need
- involving you in volunteer experiences
- mentoring
- involving you in charitable community efforts.

If you cannot identify anyone who provided this guidance for you, reflect on what inspires you to be generous. Is it a particular population or issue? Which of the above approaches is operating in that influence?

You can also identify and write about someone or multiple people in your life who you could guide or support as they develop into skillful givers.

CHAPTER 4

Generosity as a Practice

We all know people we would consider generous. The term itself
sounds complete and static, like something fully realized. Yet the
character of generosity is actually more fluid than this. What constitutes generosity varies from one person to the next, one situation to the next, and tends to keep evolving as people change.
For acts to truly be generous and to have the greatest benefit, they
must originate from altruism. These actions are unique to every
situation; for each person's circumstance, being generous means
something different.

There is no such thing as perfect generosity, no ultimate measure of success. Knowing this can liberate us from absolutist expectations. Yet it also makes generosity hard to define or chart. Many
people who others consider to be generous may not think of themselves as such because they do not have an objective measure with
which they can compare their actions. Meanwhile, there are others who may appear to exhibit generosity but do not actually put
themselves out much at all. For all these reasons, it helps to think
of generosity as an internal approach that develops and manifests
itself in the world through action. In this it is much like meditation, prayer, worship, or other religious practice. In fact, I consider
my practice of generosity to be intimately related to my spiritual
life; for me, it is a religious practice.

That is why this book is called *The Generosity Path*. As a practice, it is a way of thinking and conduct, a way of life. And as a met-

aphor it is a path to follow on a journey—it may have crossroads, places to rest, and perhaps some challenging uphill sections.

Barbara (p. 6) recalled a principle of the Jewish religion: "There is a tenet in the *Torah* that if you save one person, it is like saving the world. That doing right by one person is like doing right by everyone." And Anthony (p. 90) gave another example from Jewish theology: the term *tikkun*, which refers to humanity's shared responsibility "to restore or repair the world." The word *tikkun* is included in the *Aleinu*, a Jewish prayer that is traditionally recited three times each day. Anthony was quick to point out that one's duty in *tikkun* is not narcissistic in the sense that "the world is broken and I am the one who has the key to the restoration," but is done out of a sense that beauty and justice in the world can be restored through our shared efforts. Using this deeper approach, Anthony said he has "gratitude for all of the world's wonders as well as its brokenness."

Daniel (p. 70) came to his life of service after a spiritual retreat. During a time when he was successful in his business, he realized that his hours and attention to work were harming his relationships with his wife and children. This made him unhappy, and he felt something essential was missing. So he started reading about spirituality. This led him to go on a contemplative retreat, for prayer and reflection, without electronic communication. During the retreat, he came to cherish Benedictine concepts of hospitality, and ultimately to dedicate his life to volunteer service.

Seeing Opportunity

Practice is a time when we apply ourselves to something, as in piano practice or meditation practice. It is more about a willingness to show up regularly and do our best, and less about our ability to perform perfectly on command. It also implies taking part in a variety of activities. For instance, in meditation, we might try visualization, using a *mantra,* or just sitting quietly, paying attention to our breathing. For me, the word *practice* takes the pressure off; I am not expected it to get it exactly right every time. Yet it also calls me to be dedicated, choose to do it regularly, exercise some discipline, and look for ways to improve.

What makes you think of someone as generous? It may be the scale of what they give, as the definition states—more than is necessary or expected. It may also be that they are reliably generous, over time. When consistently practicing generosity, you are joining their ranks. You are following the example of the people who modeled generosity for you and you are modeling it for other people as a pursuit that is practiced over time.

Generosity with our money holds the greatest cultural challenge for many of us, so this book focuses particularly on the opportunities it presents. However, if taken on its own, financial generosity can become cold and unsatisfying, like a business transaction. So consider generosity with all of the resources you have available. Be generous with your eyes and your touch; welcome people and signal to them that you accept them as they are. Be generous with your skills and intelligence; work toward making this world a better place. Be generous with your heart; grow your personal relationships. Be generous with your muscle; help people when they need you to add your strength to theirs. These many ways of being generous inform each other.

> The habit of giving only enhances the desire to give.
> Walt Whitman

The practice of generosity means holding the intention to be giving in any way you can. This creates many possibilities. If you are more present with people—the most basic and possibly most profound form of generosity—then you will be more aware of their needs. And you will see opportunities to be with them in their needs or to help them. In that process, you may find ways to make financial contributions to them or others more skillfully. For instance, if you are talking to a young, unwed mother who needs help, you may hear her problems sympathetically. You may be able to give her transportation to the supermarket and back, and you may assist her financially. You may also try to affect the system she is working in by financially supporting community efforts to help young, unwed mothers. You may donate to a nonprofit organization that supports unwed mothers and get invited to one of their charitable events. In the process, you may meet more single mothers who are supported by the nonprofit, and you might be compelled to volunteer your time or skill to assist their efforts.

Elise and Barry's (p. 56) adoption of a Central American boy and support of the Central American immigrant community came about after Elise was introduced to an inspiring Catholic nun. Elise says she will never forget what the nun told her: "You can always give; there is always an opportunity at any moment. It might be just a smile or a hug, it might be that someone needs a coat, it might be food, it might be a lot of money."

Daily Practice

If your practice points to financial generosity as part of your intention over a period of time and with regular attention, then you could make it part of your daily life. Amid the challenges we face every day, this practice starts with you. Beginning your day with some fulfilling self-care will build your balance and clarity so that you are more able to address what you encounter during the day. That might be a few minutes staying in your warm, cozy bed before starting the day; it could mean prayer or meditation first thing in the morning, or a walk to see the dawning light and smell the morning air. Mornings are often times of rushing and frustration, so be gentle and create joy for yourself and your family by finding a way to be gracious. It will color the rest of your day.

Even if that is not possible, try to put habits in place so that you are reminded of your generosity practice as soon as you wake. That could be as obvious as a sign posted in the bathroom or a reminder in your work bag. No matter what the prompt is, it should remind you from the start of the day that opportunities to be generous are all around you. It doesn't have to take any time out of your routine, and it will start your day off with a good feeling. Try these messages (or make your own): "Let my generosity shine today" or "Think generously, speak generously, act generously." Daniel has a prayer he created and uses for this purpose every day: "God keep me patient, peaceful, polite, positive, prayerful, prideless, and placed."

Part of my own daily practice of generosity came from a dear friend, Sharon Groves. Some years ago, she and I had developed an eight-session seminar on financial generosity and were teaching it together. I was on a phone call with her one day, frustrated with a mutual colleague who was not acting on something I needed her to do. Sharon asked me simply, "What is the most generous response you can have to this situation?" She asked it with care and general concern, not to shame or embarrass me, so I took the question seriously. It woke me up like an alarm, helping me to respond as my best self, in a more caring and productive way, in that situation and countless other since. Now, whenever I am faced with a choice, a confrontation, or a need, I ask myself:

What is the most generous response I can make?

Whenever I am angry or puzzled or frustrated, this question helps me to get back to a generous attitude. More on using this question is covered in the Activity section at the end of this chapter.

Throughout your day, you might ask yourself this question as well, or pass it along to others. Or you may consider giving messages to yourself that you might normally give to another person. So if someone said to you, "I am just too busy and tired to do that today!" you might respond with, "Can I help? It sounds like you need some rest; do you think it can wait until tomorrow? A good night sleep will do you good." That might be a good thing to say to yourself at certain times.

This self-care is not simply to make yourself feel good. If you crave attention because you are suffering in some way, then your
text continues on page 58

ELISE AND BARRY

By giving, we blossom ten-fold.
—Elise

Although Elise and Barry are married and both successful professionals, they are very different from each other. Elise is outgoing, tall, and engaging so usually gets noticed when she enters a room. She is a nonprofit leader working to provide fair and universal access to the legal system. Barry is an artist and teacher. He is older than Elise and quite private; he did not speak often or at length during our interview. It seemed that they came from very different backgrounds and operated differently in the world.

Elise has a long-standing relationship with a nun who serves the low-income immigrant community in a rural area near where they live. Through the nun, the couple (who are both of European origin) have an adopted son of Central American heritage. During the adoption process, Elise and Barry came to learn more about the struggles in their son's immigrant community here in the United States and forged some strong relationships with them. In the end, Elise and Barry created a nonprofit to provide support and shelter to Central American single mothers and their children.

In general, Barry is much more self-contained and pragmatic than Elise. By his own account, he is not as quick to respond and give, but his response is direct and intense. He believes that one must see problems first-hand by volunteering to address them effectively with financial support. Although he seems shy around this type of direct engagement, it is valuable and motivating for him when it happens. Barry recognizes that his charitable acts provide him with the confirmation of his self-concept as a good person. He has less difficulty than Elise in accepting support. For him, being generous in specific ways creates a consonance with his values.

Elise learned in early youth how important it is to think about and respond to people who have fewer resources than she does. She tends to support many organizations that work for systemic change and responds to a compelling organizational mission; however, she is also inspired by the personal stories of people who need help. She gives financial gifts freely and as much as she can, which prompts her to worry about having enough for her family. For Elise, time is a more precious commodity than money. She struggles to allocate her time well; her family always takes priority.

Although they have strikingly different personalities with different approaches to financial generosity, Elise and Barry have found a way to work together and make profound changes in the lives of immigrant women and children. A major shift occurred for them when they adopted their cherished son. Since they have started a nonprofit, they dedicate significant time and resources to that effort—picking up donated items and storing them in their garage until they can be delivered, spending weekends as a family living with those they serve, and managing the organization. In the process, they are raising their son with values about giving and helping him to retain the culture from his birth country.

---

generosity practice will be inhibited until that is resolved. The most basic of these personal needs are summed up in the acronym HALT, which stands for hungry, angry, lonely, tired. The acronym reflects the need to stop to address what is going on. If you are experiencing any of these four states, try to do something about it as soon as you can. Then you can be more available to be generous to others.

It is a regular occurrence: When you are feeling ill or down, you run into someone who wants you to do something for them. Or just when you think you are as exhausted as you can get, you are asked to do one more thing that will not wait. You cannot always be in top readiness to be generous; yet those might be important instances you do not want to miss, and giving at those times can actually energize you and help turn you around. There are two things you can do to increase the likelihood that you will have a generous reaction in that type of situation. The first is to structure your life in a way that allows you to take the best care of yourself as possible. The second is to surround yourself with people who can support you—both in your generosity and during times when you need it. Those preparations are broader in scope, but are worth the effort. You can also train yourself in the habit of paying attention to the needs of others, despite what you may be experiencing yourself. Becoming a careful observer and growing your curiosity supports this habit.

> Expressing gratitude is somewhat like rolling a snowball down a hill. Once you set it in motion, it will grow and accelerate by itself.
>
> Zhi Gang Sha

Another way to strengthen our daily practice is to be aware of our own irritation in specific circumstances. Many people are taught social skills from an early age and know to act politely in most instances; however, our inner dialogues may be critical and judgmental. In the supermarket, we might allow someone to jump in front of us at the checkout line; yet, we might be critical of shoppers who forget something and need to go back to get it, or annoyed with a cashier who chats too much with customers. When we react solely on our irritation, we can either make sharp comments or fume internally. Neither of these reactions allows for much generous spirit, and both increase rather than alleviate our bad mood. Cultivating a choice-ful and patient approach helps. If we really do not have time to wait, we can try to find a reasonable alternative.

Gratitude

Related to this kind of self-generosity is being aware of and grateful for all we have received, all we have now, and all we will encounter every day. Our lives are a mix of the beauty, joy, love, pain, sorrow, and suffering that are fundamental to every human life. No matter what your experiences are, it is important to be grounded in the reality of your situation and to recognize the things that bring you joy and those that weigh heavily on your mind. Once you are clear about these things, be grateful for what you are experiencing.

Try to be grateful every day—it will improve your outlook and help you through many situations. Scientific studies show that being grateful may improve your well-being—help you be happier, more helpful, more forgiving, and less depressed[9]. Your gratitude may also encourage people to be more generous with you. By cultivating gratitude, and practicing so that you feel it on a regular basis, your reactions to the world around you will reflect that and help you have a more generous response. How you understand your situation will affect how you act.

If you come into any situation feeling that the world is a beautiful place and that you have been given many valuable things during your lifetime, you may feel more secure in yourself and your resources. The inner warmth you feel from this gratitude will open a channel in your heart through which gifts to other people can flow. And your presence of mind—from holding a realistic picture of where you are in relation to other people—will help you be present for the people around you and sensitive to their needs.

Anthony speaks beautifully about how his response to situations changes depending on his inner clarity, and how this leads him to the deeper levels of joy in giving:

> Sometimes when I am asked to give, I am caught off-guard and I just wind up responding to someone without thinking; that is not such a good feeling. Sometimes giving is the right thing to do and I feel good about that; it is like a spiritual discipline. And then at the richest end of the spectrum, I sometimes feel, "Giving is what I am *meant* to be doing in this moment"; I feel this at the deepest level.

To develop your generosity and stabilize your daily practice, remember that in spite of its problems this planet is an incredible gift to us all. It provides sustenance, sensual pleasure, and infinite variety. We are surrounded by this beauty, which is ever-changing and recurring, so we can experience familiar pleasures repeatedly. That is just as unavoidable as suffering, and these two opposites create the great balance of life. Our birth was a fortunate gift from our parents and whatever spark of life (God, Yahweh, Allah, whatever you believe) that supported that conception. Our bodies and minds are miraculous systems that allow us to create, understand, calculate, and dream. In fact, each person is born with the ability to seek and find satisfaction, no matter their circumstances. Without reason or cause, people love us and we love other people. This love can take myriad forms, including friendship, parenthood, and the enduring affection of marriage or partnership. We are the beneficiaries of generations of inventors and designers who have created wonderful processes and objects; these make our lives easier, more comfortable, and more pleasurable. Millions of thinkers and teachers have gone before us, and we are the inheritors of that knowledge.

In addition to what we have inherited or been given regardless of merit, we can also be grateful for what we have been able to achieve in this life. Whether it is getting a high school diploma, reaching a sports goal, succeeding in a business, or having a baby, you have realized your achievements. You have earned them, worked for them, or created them; you have made them happen. For whatever reason, you were able to break through the barriers that stood between you and that goal to achieve success. Whatever comforts and security you have created for yourself may be a source of joy for you and help you feel more confident in your giving. Some of these achievements may also have resulted in resources that can now be tapped for your giving.

In her interview, Liz (p. 174) was concerned that we who live in the United States might lose our appreciation for all we have in this nation: "If you lose the sense of how much you have, you lose the sense of how to secure it, how to promote it, and how to reach out to other people."

Ups and Downs

Of course, for some people, life does not offer a good balance. Some of us are born into terrible situations of unavoidable suffering. In some cases, these situations seem impossible, or actually are impossible, to escape. Even if that is not the situation, sometimes life is going along beautifully and we make terrible mistakes, or something happens that we neither caused nor could control, and it feels like our lives are ruined. For

> The amount you give isn't important.
> What matters is what that amount represents in terms of your life.
>
> Jim Rohn

many, only faith or hopefulness keeps them going. Others do not have a developed faith to rely on and they cave in to despair, or treat themselves or others badly. Self-care and gratitude practices will not only help you through your challenging times, they will help you remain generous to those around you as well.

As with any practice, there will be ups and downs in being intentionally generous. Because of things going on in your life, there will be times when you keep your blinders on and reduce some of your engagement until you get through a personal or professional challenge. Remember that a practice is about continuity over time, which can allow for short breaks if you need them. While you may need to set it aside for a short time and then come back to it, you will still move forward. Just come back to it and take up the practice again.

Because Henry (pg. 136) has been practicing generosity for so long, he has had significant ups and downs and has good advice about sticking with it:

> You are going to have some setbacks. You will say, "Wow, that was a waste of money," or, "I cannot believe I spent a whole day on that." So just keep in mind your other experiences. Or maybe you are in the wrong place, the wrong position, and you need to explore other options. Maybe you are working for or donating to the wrong organization—but do not stop! Do not assume that every experience will result in a positive or a negative result.

One of the most wonderful things about all practices is that they grow and change, even without our intentions. As we develop, we reach thresholds that we may have not seen before or even considered. Once we cross those thresholds, the view is different, and so is our experience. A practice is made up of actions oriented toward making a change in yourself, sometimes reaching deep levels, so there are no defined steps to follow. These thresholds can neither be planned nor prepared for—except by heading in a chosen direction, learning as we go, and doing the best we can. Sometimes we find guides for these transitions, people to accompany us on the way; yet sometimes we must follow our own instincts. This growth will not benefit from rigidly or punitively enforcing our inner messages. You are on a path. Try to enjoy the journey!

PRACTICES

Green String Generosity

A string tied around the wrist is used in many religions. It often represents protection from evil forces, a good-luck charm, and a blessing that is carried by the receiver. Wearing a red string is a custom practiced in Kabbalah tradition of Judaism, in order to ward off misfortune brought about by an "evil eye." In a Buddhist ceremony, a white string is tied on the wrist to call a spirit back into a soul; the string ensures that the spirit will remain in that body. In Thailand people use string bracelets as part of wedding and funeral ceremonies. Tying string on the wrist is part of both the Theravada and Tibetan Buddhist traditions. They consider it protection because it reminds the wearer of the Buddha and his teachings.

In the case of this particular practice, tying a string to your wrist is not religious; it is to remind you to be generous.

Challenge yourself to do these three things:

1. Tie a piece of green string, ribbon, or yarn on the wrist of your dominant hand to remind you to be generous every day, in every situation, as you give and receive.
2. Let it remind you to ask: *What is the most generous response I can make?* The green string should remind you to always to ask this whenever you are faced with a choice, confrontation, or need.
3. Invite your loved ones and friends to join you in wearing the green string. See how much generosity you can generate!

Journaling

At the end of every day, sit quietly for a few minutes and take an inventory of how generous you were that day. Briefly review your day in your mind and see if any situations pop up. Here are some sample questions to ask yourself, if you choose. Do not make it too complicated or time-consuming; just respond to one or two of these questions.

- Have I given freely and where needed?
- Have I consciously and graciously received?
- Have I been consistent in expressing myself to those I love and care for?
- Have I appreciated others?
- Have I shared myself and my gifts in my community?
- Have I noticed and acknowledged the generosity in people around me?

CHAPTER 5

Risks and Barriers

As desirable as generosity is, there are some concerns that arise when people set out to be more financially generous. Although you may not encounter them, foreseeing and being prepared for these potential challenges may make them less daunting and help you continue to develop your generosity.

Future chapters will cover various approaches and tools to help build your skillfulness and personal sustainability as a giver. These will help ensure that you avert risks, that your generous impulses and resources are well-received, and that your giving makes a difference—which will support you in giving even more boldly. Still, if you do confront a barrier or take a risk, it might mean you are leaping forward in developing your generosity. As Joan Halifax, the Buddhist teacher, says about the early stages of a meditation practice, which might apply to generosity as well, "I tell you, to stop in this world is to create the conditions where a lot of unusual experiences can rise up. So be very respectful of your situation and proceed with love and with care, as well as courage."[10]

The people whose stories are included in this book feared pitfalls; yet they encountered only minor incidents that did not prevent their continuing generosity. In this chapter, you will see real examples where people actually ran into trouble. Take these as manageable and instructive forewarnings and don't let them deter you, because being generous holds deep and rich rewards. If we prepare ourselves and proceed intelligently, the actual risks are relatively rare. Our capacity grows with our experience.

Common Barriers

Perhaps the most basic of all impediments to giving was identified by Bill Gates, chairman of the Microsoft Corporation, at his speech for the Harvard University commencement in 2007:[11] "All of us here in this Yard, at one time or another, have seen human tragedies that broke our hearts, and yet we did nothing—not because we didn't care, but because we didn't know what to do. If we had known how to help, we would have acted." It is hard to know how to be effective in making a difference with our generosity, especially when the issues and our lives can be so complex. The primary impulse to make a difference is a powerful opening and can fuel later efforts. Part of our work in developing the capacity to give is to find out how to be most effective with our resources in creating positive change. We need to cut through the complexity of information to gain clarity and understanding about the problem.

> A society that encourages us to break open the shell of selfishness and self-centeredness contains the seeds of a society where people are honest, truthful and loving. . . . Each one of us, I believe, is on a journey towards this openness where we risk to love.
>
> Jean Vanier

The most commonly mentioned obstacle to generosity is the same one that inhibits us from doing all kinds of things in our lives: the lack of free or flexible time. If we rule out opportunities for giving due to time constraints, our schedule becomes a broad obstruction to generosity. Generosity requires us to slow down and notice our surroundings; it takes attention and patience. It involves stepping out of our normal routines, noticing the needs of others, figuring out how to help, and then expending more resources to help. This applies whether we are holding the door for someone, giving someone directions, or making a thoughtful donation to a charitable organization. With the luxury of time to waste, these seem like insignificant acts. But if we are late for a meeting, giving someone a parking spot might make us even later. On top of this, we may not give ourselves enough time to fulfill our own needs. That may make it very difficult to give time to someone else. Elise (p. 56) expresses this feeling with hurried exasperation,

I am a full-time mom, we run a nonprofit, I am a wife, and I am running a complex program at work. I have no time to be more generous. Physically, I just do not have the time. Time with my family is so precious, it is such an asset and it is so fleeting, and that is a barrier to my generosity.

Many people who are busy with jobs and families also volunteer their time and skills to work for important social change. How do they do it? If something is important to you, you can find the time for it; setting priorities can help. Getting control of your schedule as much as possible, so that you are making active choices, will free up time for intentional giving. Why do people regularly volunteer when they are already so busy? Obviously, they find it compelling or gratifying.

Two basic approaches to generosity will help with the issue of limited time. The first is simple: Do what you can where you are, with the resources you have at hand. This does not require you to add to your to-do list, impinge on your schedule, or make a lot of preparation. It does oblige you to be mindful and notice things going on around you with an eye toward generosity, so you don't miss opportunities. The second approach is to create a philanthropic plan in advance and implement it as you go along. This takes some time at the outset; after that, it should reduce the amount of time you spend. More on this planning is included later in the book.

Certain fears may impede your practice of giving. Elise and Barry (p. 56) both feared that giving too much would leave their family without what they need. They felt as many people do—that expanding your generosity is like opening up a fire hydrant on the street: the gushing surge of water would be hard to control. Without monitoring the flow, before you know it, all your resources can pour out. This is actually a double concern: One is that you may not have enough for yourself and your family so cannot afford this largesse. The other is not feeling able to set and hold reasonable personal boundaries: If you engage with people or an issue you will not be able to stop trying to help them. In the end, you will disregard your own budget constraints. Elise said,

> The most obvious worry is the physical act of giving away all of your money and not being able to meet your bills every month. . . . I tend to write most of the checks and need to make sure I am not putting my family at risk in any way, extending myself into a place where they would feel discomfort. I have never done that and admire people who say that they have given everything up. I think that must be amazingly freeing but also terrifying.

Elise manages this in the way you might: She finds a balance her family can live with between what they need for their own use, and what they can give to others. Elise knows what her family reasonably needs, and she creates a budget for her charitable giving. Once that budget is expended, she considers additional requests one at a time, in the context of her overall finances. You can do this yourself by gathering financial statements of earnings, holdings, expenditures, and donations so that you are clear about limits in your financial life (see Chapter 6).

Someone who is "overly" financially generous might fear not having enough in case of unemployment or family illness. This does happen to some people. In the early twentieth century, Owen D. Young was the president of General Electric, and went on to be a founder of the Radio Corporation of America and NBC. He became a nationally prominent figure and went on to counsel five U.S. presidents. Young made huge charitable commitments to various institutions. And then the Great Depression came, decimating his wealth so that he owed more in charitable commitments than his net worth. Still, he decided to uphold his pledges, although this meant that he and his family had to change their lifestyle and move to a farm. Young remained influential, but he never regained his former level of wealth, and it took the rest of his life to fulfill his charitable pledges.[12]

Although this story is extreme because of the drastic lifestyle change this family experienced, we should remember three things. First, many people were financially devastated and had a complete change in the way they were living during the Great Depression; the Young family actually fared better than many. Second, the Youngs were never homeless or hungry, nor missed out on education or access to good healthcare while Owen Young fulfilled his pledges. Finally, we cannot know or calculate the benefits, the meaning, and personal satisfaction that Young gained from completing his gift pledges to those organizations. Remember that any financial commitment you make to a charitable organization is not a legally binding contract. You can always reduce or cancel the commitment if you need to.

Fear about giving too much is often based on anxiety about unforeseeable events in the future. Barry states this directly: "What is a barrier to financial generosity? Hoarding it, not wanting to give it away, wanting to keep it close to home with my family, fears that I will be needy in the future."

Forecasters may "predict" unforeseeable disastrous events in finance, the environment, politics, or warfare. Politicians and the media, for their own purposes, may describe the social service and public welfare systems as being in jeopardy. Some of these predictions may be reasonable and actually provide direction for your saving and giving plans. You must use good judgment to discern exaggeration from reasonable projections. As you go through that decision-making process, remember that many of these warnings are given with the assumption that your money is the key to all

text continues on page 72

DANIEL

There are two reasons to be generous: people need help, and it is good for you spiritually.

—*Daniel*

Daniel is a man at peace; he is relaxed, quiet, and calm. We met in the fellowship hall of the church where he worships with his family. In middle age, he is a full-time volunteer. Three mornings a week he cooks for a food charity, the other two days he is the custodian and property manager at the church where we met. He also works in the garden of another religious building. He coaches his son's soccer team and is looking to fill the remainder of his week providing recreational therapy for people with cognitive impairments.

Daniel was once successful in business. Early in his career, he joined a small company that supported the financial services industry and later became a partner in the firm. Through taking advantage of business opportunities and holding themselves to high work standards, the company grew exponentially with matching increases of revenue. At the peak of his time there, Daniel was working seven days a week for up to fifteen hours each day. However, along with this schedule, Daniel no longer had time to volunteer at his church and other charities, so he and his wife intentionally set up a giving plan and increased their charitable giving to compensate.

Eventually, his work consumed him. It woke him up in the middle of the night; he thought about work when he was with his kids at the playground on Saturday. This level of stress damaged both his health and personality. He had a bad temper and little patience, and he realized he was often complaining. His work was no longer fun. And it no longer had the excitement of growth; he was just trying to make sure the "wheels didn't come off." His wife suggested that he quit and find something else to do.

During this time, he used to go to a local coffee shop with his children on Saturday mornings. One of the regulars there, a near-stranger, became hospitalized with no other caregivers, and Daniel stepped in to help. The project helped him bond with his son, and eventually it transformed his perspective and priorities. Growing out of this opening, Daniel went on a spiritual retreat that led to his leaving his company and dedicating himself to a life of full-time volunteer service. Although this transformation took years, it created a radical shift in his life.

Daniel credits his wife with introducing him to charitable giving, encouraging him to volunteer, and supporting him during this transition—saying that they work as a team as much as a couple. Daniel's occupations allow him to be fully present with his children. And, at the time of our meeting, Daniel's spiritual practice, life of service, and resources all seem to be aligned.

---

aspects of your well-being. This ignores the fact that other sources of support will probably be available to you, such as public support systems, close family relationships, and active participation from your community; you can intentionally cultivate these last two to prepare for the future. No matter how much you give, you cannot lose your intelligence, your good heart, your knowledge, and your skills by sharing them with others—these will always provide you with a level of power and control. You can rely on your character, human relationships, and inner resources to ensure your future well-being.

More foreseeable challenges include aging, which for almost everyone involves concern about losing our ability to be independent and having enough resources for the support we may need. Our average lifespan is increasing and the possibility of long-term illness is unpredictable. For younger people, this means preparing for more extended periods of later life and possibly chronic illness during a time of a fixed and limited income. Being financially generous in the face of the unknown takes planning and saving, being willing to adjust later in life, and faith in things besides money. I learned valuable lessons in this regard early in my professional life when I worked with elders in financial-assistance housing. None of these older people had the level of resources we all think we will want and need late in our lives. Many of them had some form of physical disability. Yet those who were connected socially in their community and participated in satisfying, meaningful activities seemed happy. They supported each other and although they were not financially carefree, other factors seemed more important to them.

When developing generosity and creating consistency in your giving, a sense of urgency can be a powerful motivator. Yet impatience, which is a different state of being, can act as a barrier. Although impatience relates to a perceived lack of time, it is also an internal state distinct from eagerness. I am, by nature, an energetic person who prefers a fast pace in physical motion, in thinking, and in working on projects. Part of my maturation has been to develop more patience, and I have found this has supported my generosity in innumerable ways.

For generosity, patience and the ability to give persistent attention are essential—with oneself, with charitable systems, and with people you hope to benefit. They are especially necessary for problems that require our support on an ongoing basis, including what might be considered unmeetable needs. Here is where a practice for generosity fits well with the needs of the world. You give in an

> If each retained possession only of what he needed, no one would be in want and all would live in contentment.
>
> Mahatma Gandhi

enduring way, and the needs you're trying to address may be long-lasting as well. Issues such as childhood hunger, tropical diseases, or global warming resist substantive improvement so intensely that they have been around for many years and will probably endure long after our generation is gone. We should make every effort to address these problems, yet our expectations should be realistic and adjusted to these types of issues.

Some people who give charitably do not have the patience for enduring or intractable issues. They want swift and obvious results, or to be part of a comprehensive solution. They may believe that their hope and insistence can completely eradicate a problem. There is much to be said for this determination. If you have this temperament, find causes to support that match your need for completion. And be mindful that an enduring practice of generosity may challenge you.

If we are willing to have the patience to keep supporting a special population with intractable needs, it may help improve their long-term efficacy. In some instances, a person in need might be trying to solve their problems but they are not yet able to do so, or it will take a long time. Or the person to whom you are giving will always need that generosity because of a disability, medical condition, or deep psychological wound. In these cases, if we give our support expecting that it will change them and they will not need our generosity again, our expectation might be unhelpful and indeed might add to their challenges. A part of generosity involves allowing people to change according to their own capabilities and in a time frame they determine themselves, which means they might need repeated support. Your expectations will influence how patient you can be when trying to affect change. Setting informed and reasonable goals early on should help with this.

Even if we are patient and stalwart, we all run the risk of compassion fatigue (or, in financial giving, donor fatigue). This burnout may cause us to feel numb. Aside from self-care, one thing that helps with this is understanding or refining our interpersonal boundaries—remaining aware that the sufferings of others are separate from our own. We are not the only "heroes." Many people contribute to making this a better world. This allows us to be more able to sustain our efforts and provide more help. In her poem "Natural Resources," Adrienne Rich writes,[13]

My heart is moved by all I cannot save:
so much has been destroyed

I have to cast my lot with those
who age after age, perversely,

with no extraordinary power,
reconstitute the world.

As with any other interaction, being generous with a person or organization sometimes works out beautifully. Sometimes it feels like it was meant to be, and every part is satisfying. And sometimes, just trying to be generous is challenging from the outset. It is awkward, it brings disappointments and fuels doubts; it feels like a failure. Don't let that stop you. If something goes wrong, if someone irritates you, if you seem to be blocked from accomplishing your goals, try to take a lighter approach and forgive your own missteps. These are great opportunities for generosity to others and yourself. These "negative" emotions are a signal, like a flag going up, to show that something has to change, or to show where generosity might be applied. Your generous impulse is true, and your passion is valuable. Stick with it and find a way that will work for you and for your cause. That may mean trying again, taking a different approach, finding a different organization, or contributing in a new way. Remind yourself of your good experiences and let them inform your actions when challenges arise. Do not give up on your hopes. As long as you are willing to continue your attempts, your generosity will help you find a way to make the difference you seek. Of course, when you feel good and things around you are going swimmingly, it is easier to be open and generous, so don't miss those opportunities either.

As you expand your generosity, you may be concerned about the consequences. Perhaps you have already encountered hazards when altering your approach to giving. When you decide to shift your understanding of how to use your resources and begin using them to fulfill your personal mission, you step into new territory. Expect some missteps; your points of reference may require some reorientation. Following your passion or "calling" opens unexpected doors. These can be delightful experiences, yet they can be disconcerting. Having some forethought about possible risks might help you traverse these thresholds.

Your own misgivings or doubt may at times stand in your way. These may be sparked by an interaction, like someone or some organization continuing to ask you for resources to a point that makes you uncomfortable. This may confirm a fear that they may not leave you alone and may even offend you in their aggressiveness. This is a real concern, and it actually happens, as it did to me once. A professional caller asking for donations was so aggressive and relentless in their "pitch" that I asked them never to call me again. Your own worry about wasting money or being taken advantage of, may make you overly suspicious about nonprofits mismanaging their funds, or even acting wrongfully and illegally. This, again, is a fear with some basis in real stories that have appeared in the media, yet are very rare. Some basic checking will usually allay these fears and allow you to regain your confidence. To do this, avoid giving impulsively and gather as much information as you need before making gift decisions. In most instances, your engagement and experience with nonprofit organizations will help you to feel confident in your efforts and be able to fend off unwanted approaches. In chapter 8, you will find resources for researching nonprofits, so you can look up any organization to see that they are authentic, qualified, and effective.

Connection Can Be Scary

At its most personal level, generosity is about being present with other people. Although this may seem easy, it can be demanding. Have you ever sat and gazed into the eyes of a friend or loved one, just looking to see them? Aside from people who are newly in love, this is rare, and—if you try it— demanding. Now, if you try this exercise with someone you do not know well, someone very different from you, it becomes extremely challenging. It's so simple, and so human, but it is a risk: You do not know what that person might express and what you may reveal about yourself through your eyes—the "soul's window." However, if you can really be present for someone, then that connection will be a generous one, regardless of whether you are able to provide the help they need. This is true with your spouse or partner, a relative, a friend, a colleague, or a stranger. If the person feels seen and heard by you, they will feel honored in the process.

You take a chance when you interact with people you do not know, people who may hold different norms for behavior or cultural values. Barry provided the perfect euphemism for this concern about people we do not know who have unknown qualities: *spooky others.* He said, "I believe that I am most generous when I get over the hurdle of dealing with 'spooky' others."

Consider exchanges with people asking for money on the street. This is an exaggerated example of an interaction between people at different socioeconomic levels. Some pedestrians are bothered by people asking for money on the street because they are not sure what to do—give them money, or even try to interact with them. Some people are frightened of others who look like they live on the street because they may display behaviors that indicate they have either mental illness or substance-abuse problems. And there is a possibility, after all, that they may want to engage with you more than you can handle. What if they want to come home with you, come back to your office, or want you to accompany them somewhere? What if they really told you all about their troubles in detail? What if they then asked you

> To be generous means . . . to redefine our boundaries. For the generous person, borders are permeable. What is yours—your suffering, your problems—is also mine: This is compassion. What is mine—my possessions, my body, my knowledge and abilities, my time and resources, my energy—is also yours: This is generosity.
>
> Pierro Ferucci

to do something very time-consuming or to give them a substantial amount of money? What if they wanted to forge a personal relationship with you—would you welcome that?

In 2008 Duke Helfand of the *Los Angeles Times* reported on the B'nai David-Judea Synagogue's challenges in assisting a group of people who did not have their own housing.[14] The synagogue has a program to give supermarket gift cards out to people who need them. However, the supply is never enough for the number of people who need it. Some recipients began sleeping in the synagogue's doorway in order to be among the first to get a supermarket card. Eventually, some people had to be told that they would not receive the assistance if they kept blocking the doorway. The congregation had to balance its desire to be charitable with setting appropriate boundaries so that it could continue functioning.

Helfand also found out personally how hard it is to strike that balance. While writing the story, he gave his cell phone number to a person he was interviewing who frequented the synagogue's program. A few nights later, that person called asking for money, and Helfand realized the man was calling from within his own neighborhood. For Helfand, who wondered about how safe it might be to expose a stranger to his family, this was too close for comfort. It is important to step with mindfulness, caution, and appropriate pacing into these types of relationships. At the same time, we must not assume that people are dangerous because they have material, psychological, or social needs that are not being met. There is great injustice in the world against people from marginalized groups; part of our generosity may include dropping our biases and seeking authentic fellowship with those we hope to help.

Priorities and Balance

As you consider your resources, and how they might be reallocated to accommodate more giving, try not to eliminate anything from your life that brings you deeper meaning and nurtures important relationships. Still, as you make changes in your life around generosity, it may cause your personal relationships to change in significant ways. The best way to deal with this may be to communicate your hopes, plans, and dreams with people who are important to you and to hear their responses directly. That way, the people in your life have a chance to adjust their expectations. This kind of communication may also open the door for others to join you on your new path.

Sometimes families can experience conflict when they don't all agree about the allocation of resources for charitable purposes. The Mondavi wine-making family went through an exaggerated and public example of this. Robert Mondavi, the family's charismatic and visionary leader, helped to found an educational wine and food center at the University of California, and made sizable donations to it. These gifts were supported with stock from the family business, Mondavi Winery, and the gifts threatened its solvency. This spurred a family conflict so intense that the Mondavi board eventually took control of the company away from them and sold it.[15] This kind of problem might be avoided with good communication and agreement within your family or community members, so that decisions about charitable gifts are agreed upon and supported broadly.

Satisfaction Isn't Guaranteed

A final risk regarding generosity is that you will not gain the satisfaction you seek. Your alternative may be to spend money on yourself and your family, surrounding yourself or doing things that you know make you feel good. If you know you love gourmet food, you can be fairly certain that you will enjoy dinner in a favorite fancy restaurant. Amy-Lee (p. 108) commented, "It is about understanding the difference between needs and wants. People neglect to give money to causes because they want more money in their pocket for their own spending; they are not saving for other reasons." There is no guarantee that donating money for a new water system somewhere in Africa, or toward rebuilding the Ninth Ward in New Orleans, or sponsoring a South American child's operation will make you feel as good as spending money on yourself. Although it may sound ridiculous on the surface to compare the two types of spending, they represent the breadth of choices you have in using your resources. When you donate money, you are gambling that benefiting others, and making a difference in the world, will create deeper or longer-lasting satisfaction for you than spending money on yourself. Social economic research and the experiences of this book's interviewees indicate that this is a good bet.

This chapter has laid out some fears, challenges, and actual risks you may encounter in your practice of being generous. Despite all of this, Daniel (p. 70) reminds us that the potential benefits of increased giving far outweigh the risks:

> I have never had a negative experience from giving more money or time to a person or group that needs it. I am sure they are out there, but the positives must outweigh the negatives.

PRACTICES

Assessing Our Connections to Others
This exercise, adapted from the Buddhist practitioner Pema Chödrön, is intended to help us see our usual surroundings in new ways so that we can notice our reactions and availability to others.

Walk slowly down a block that is well-traveled by different kinds of people; not a residential street or one where you will know most of the people (if you live in a rural area, do this when you next visit a larger community). Try to stay as "awake" as possible to whoever you see. As you pass people, simply notice whether your inclination is to open up to them, ignore them, or avoid them altogether. Notice if you are feeling attraction, aversion, or indifference, without adding self-judgment. You might feel compassion toward someone who looks depressed or cheered by someone who's smiling to herself. You might feel fear and aversion to someone else. After you have done this exercise, write down what you noticed about your own reactions.

Give Away a Dollar
Building on the practice above, take one dollar this week and give it away. You may give change or bills regularly to people in need; this time, try to be as open and present to the person you are giving it to as possible. Give it in a way that seems deeply generous to you, not built on guilt, impulsiveness, or compulsion but out of as clear a sense of generosity as you can muster. Write about the experience.

Journaling
Think of a time in the past week or two when you were not generous, for whatever reason. Try to set aside any self-criticism; see if you can identify the underlying reason for the lack of generosity and write about it. In the coming week, be aware of that reaction and see if you can adjust it to be more generous.

If you are not sure what an underlying reason might be, consider this example from my own experience. A friend recently asked me in an email to make a charitable gift to a nonprofit. I know that a number of her family members suffer from a medical condition that the nonprofit works to alleviate, and how important the issue is to my friend. Still, I dismissed it because this gift would not fit into my charitable priorities or planning. Upon reflection, I realized that my reaction came more from the fact that in my professional life, I had recently done a sizable amount of work and had not received payment. Although this did not put me in serious financial jeopardy, it did make me worry about my finances and affect my mood as well. My uncertainty and grumpiness led me to not consider my friend's request. Regardless of whether I had decided to make a donation, it reduced my generosity.

CHAPTER 6

Developing and Sustaining the Giver

You now have a good background on generosity, both in receiving and giving. And you have been advised of the potential barriers and risks of being more ambitious with your generosity. This chapter addresses developing your capacity to be generous while answering some of the concerns presented in the previous chapter. It includes suggestions for how to step into financial generosity sustainably—in a way that can reinvigorate you, so the practice does not become overwhelming or exhaust your personal resources.

Starting Capacity

Daniel (p. 70) knows what it is like to have limited resources, in money, time, and energy. He recommends that whatever you are contemplating, you should jump right in:

> People get overwhelmed by problems. Well, you do not have to solve the problem; just get in there and help. Do whatever you can. If something scares you, do something else. Whatever your skills are, do that thing.

Practicing generosity is not like the other activities you do; it is unlike office work or household chores. It is work of the heart and spirit, potentially life-changing and even world-changing work. It does not take place on a rigid schedule. Sometimes it may feel as if being generous is just one more of many things for which you do not have time. Yet it is easier to integrate than you might imagine, and it will put you in good spirits.

Anthony (p. 90) points out that it's best to start out with manageable goals:

> Whatever I can do, whether it is sitting with someone or writing a check, there is a sense that at least it is a small dent. That gives me a great sense of freedom. It is too daunting for me to think about something as grand as "generosity," so instead I think, "What can I actually do?"

The *Times Colonist* newspaper in Victoria, British Columbia, published a wonderful story about a janitor at the University of Victoria in Canada. Greig Cosier has serious learning disabilities that prevented him from completing high school. He worked as a night custodian in the university science building for many years and would speak with the grad students who were there working late into the night on their studies. As they were also often short on money, he would press gifts on them until, at the suggestion of one of them, he created the Custodian's Trophy.[16] He awarded this to the student he most often saw burning the midnight oil. He funded the trophy and two other awards from his custodian's salary, including a stipend and an awards dinner for twelve at a restaurant. He has made generations of friends—intelligent and learned scientists. When asked how he has done this, he responded, "I save up; it makes me feel good." Cosier spent enough time close to the students to understand not only their aspirations, but their struggles and needs. He was able, even with his modest salary, to connect with them and to give

> The practice of generosity is about creating space. We see our limits and we extend them continuously, which creates an expansiveness and spaciousness of mind that's deeply composed.
>
> Sharon Salzburg

them something that made a real difference in their lives. And just imagine the lessons he has taught them about being generous and charitable!

Cosier did not go out of his way or make a special effort to see what was needed; he just noticed things in his daily work life. The students were literally in his way as he tried to work, and yet they also enlivened what would otherwise be a lonely task. He heard them when they talked about their lives and took note of their needs. And he built his connections to them over time, knowing best the ones who were there the most. Thus, his trophy turned their arduous work and persistence into something valuable, regardless of whether their studies led to scientific success.

Once you step into becoming more giving, your generosity can develop as you go—which is why the path metaphor is so prominent throughout this book. Our capacity and skill in giving and receiving evolve as we step forward. As with other aspects of development, you may find that when you cross a threshold of experience—for instance, when you commit to giving an amount regularly instead of sporadically—your understanding and experience change as well. It's like being in a dark and unremarkable hallway. Stepping through a half-opened door, you find yourself in a spacious, light-filled room that holds beautiful things to enjoy. This brings you experiences and ideas that you could never have imagined standing in the hall; it changes your mental map. Similarly, when you grow through your experiences with being generous, you can turn back, yet you cannot unlearn this new knowledge you have gained.

Developing Your Stride

Both allowing your giving to develop and pacing yourself will help with your concerns about capacity and time limitations. You might find it motivating to use your journal to note your progress and achievements. You may also discover opportunities to mark your growth if you belong to a community that involves a giving component. Rita (p. 26) grew up in a family that always gave to their church, and she continued the practice into adulthood. She equates this growing and opening up to her spiritual growth:

> I would say that I had a gradual spiritual development. It started with a requirement where I was honoring a financial commitment to our church, where it later became ingrained. Then I wanted to give. Now I find that I give where I see the need. The more I give, the more my ability to give increases; it just becomes easier to do. Maybe it comes from your life maturing. It was hard to give generously, and now it is much easier—partially because we have more resources now, but mentally and emotionally it has become easier to do as well.

Note how Rita points to our capabilities changing at different stages of our lives. Rita developed in this way partly because she undertook actions about which she was initially uncertain. In another part of the interview, she described a situation where an organization to which she is connected put out a request to house an intern. Rita and Jim (p. 26) knew they had the room for someone else to stay, yet they hesitated because they knew they would be giving up some freedom and comfort in the process. In the end, they decided to host the intern. While he was living there, Jim and Rita realized it was less taxing than they thought and, in fact, they felt some real benefits to having him there.

Anthony's and Henry's (p. 136) giving also developed and changed with time, as their circumstances, maturity, and the quantity of their resources changed. Their efforts became more focused while they were able to disburse more resources, yet they also felt a sense of better balance. Barbara's (p. 6) path progressed from a childhood with scant family resources to young adulthood and being able to give only her hospitality, and on to a period when she is able to give financially and provide hospitality at a greater scale, and in which she even helped found a community center that will benefit people she may never meet. This maturity seems to move naturally to being more and more open-handed and benefiting more and more people in the process.

Part of stepping into a new practice inevitably means making some mistakes, and learning from the experience. If you can enter the practice graciously, and are willing to do it imperfectly, this will help retain your energy. In making small missteps, you may develop greater sensitivity and understanding, and become more emboldened to take risks again.

Rita seems to be a naturally joyful person. She told how she went out of her way to be generous, yet her lack of knowledge meant part of her gift was off the mark. She handled this with lightness and without self-criticism:

> In high school I used to volunteer in a nursing home. I would sometimes buy things for the residents, using money from my babysitting jobs; I remember buying apples and bananas, sweaters and toiletries. For some reason that I could not understand, the bananas went fast and the apples were always left. Later, I realized that their teeth would not allow them to eat the whole apples!

Sometimes, generosity grows out of a lack of response. A newspaper in Ontario, Canada, reported that when fire damaged a neighboring restaurant, Kevin and Kathy Anyan were the first to offer help to the business owner, Nik Klummer. The Anyans did this because, about ten years before, their business was also fire-damaged. Kevin Anyan recounted, "A lot of people said, 'It's terrible,' but nobody said, 'What can we do to help right now?' Being that I've walked in his shoes, I thought I should do what wasn't done for me." The Anyans offered to share their kitchen space and gave Klummer space for the supplies he could save from the fire so that he could continue with some of his catering work. This is another example of people finding a way to support others with only a minor inconvenience, as the Anyans' business was able to keep functioning while they helped Klummer work and earn money.[17]

Enough

Do you believe that if we pull together, there will be enough for everyone to have at least the basic things they need? Or do you believe there are not enough resources for everyone and that we will always have to fight for our share? Having faith in *enough* may have been challenged by experiences in your past or may make you fear the future. Or that faith may have been bolstered by an inspiration in nature, from a specific religious tradition, or having the experiences of other people being reliable and generous to you. Nearly everyone has an underlying belief in scarcity or adequacy, regardless of their wealth or poverty. Intentional generosity requires you to open your heart and hands in a way that activates your belief in *enough* or at least helps you *acts as if* you believe that there is enough for you. With experience, you may find that you have more and can afford to give more than you realized. Your confidence may grow, give you some ease, and inspire you to give more. Along the way, it is important that you find a balance you can live with between what you decide you need for your own use, and what you can give to others.

The two primary categories from which people consider giving are money and time—time includes the giving of skills, intelligence, experience, or physical activity. Depending on your circumstance, stage of life, and set of resources, you may have a lot of both of these, few of either, or some other combination. Daniel tried to be a generous giver while moving through different periods of resourcefulness in his life. When he owned a business and worked long and stressful hours, he gave significant amounts of money, in part because he longed to do something and did not have the time. Later, his time became more flexible and he was able to give moderate amounts of both. During this transition, he proceeded with caution because he and his wife had two young children and could not endanger their welfare. In contemplating leaving his employment, he asked himself, "If I were making minimum wage, could I do this? I have responsibilities and need a certain amount of income." When I interviewed him, his life had swung to the other extreme, where his income had been somewhat reduced. Yet, he was spending his life as a full-time volunteer. Daniel gave from the resource pool he had during each of these periods. He was generous in each; they took different forms, and each was sustainable for him.

Daniel's is an unusual story. He earned enough money earlier in his life so that he could help support his family, and he dedicates his time to being generous: volunteering and bettering the lives of other people. His story is unique because he made a leap into a generous life, while most of us can only make smaller changes. However, he has struggled with the same issues that many people do—questioning how much he could give, facing fears that his choices would leave his family without the resources that they might need, wondering if his efforts would make a substantial difference. Yet his previous lifestyle did not fulfill him and harmed the people he loved the most, so he followed his intuition and intentionally made huge changes in his life. Most of us will never be able to make this kind of change, yet Daniel's boldness has a lesson for each of us: that we can reach farther and be more generous than we imagine. It just takes courage.

If we are going to be ambitious in our efforts to make the world a better place, we will need to create a balance of our own needs with those of others. When we have an imbalance between giving and receiving, we can experience burnout. If we are invested in giving all the time, we may be preventing others from giving to us. Think what we might be missing! Receiving is about being generous with ourselves. In addition to allowing others to care for you when you need it, give yourself time to recharge and to experience the things that you find enriching. If you give to the point where you are denying or neglecting your own needs, then your gifts will be colored with that imbalance. Your efforts or gifts may not provide as much benefit to the recipients as you might hope. It is important to be receptive while you are giving—let those to whom who you are giving teach you lessons about receiving.

text continues on page 92

ANTHONY

It is too daunting for me to think about something as grand as "generosity," so instead I think, "What can I actually do?"
—Anthony

Anthony is truly humble. Although he was a successful consultant and author who had recently taken a high-level job with a large corporation, he exudes calmness and speaks quietly. We met during the day in a quiet restaurant where he greeted all the staff by name, and they in turn treated him like a long-lost relative. Anthony is remarkable for his attentiveness to those around him. This quiet presence and attentiveness came about through many years of striving. His challenge was to find balance with the amount of caring he felt compelled to do, while he often got to a point of being drained and needing care himself.

Coming from a Catholic Italian family of modest means, he does not remember ever discussing being charitable or generous. It was more "routine" that his parents made financial contributions to their church, even in hard times. But his mother gave freely of her time and attention, and their home was a destination for people in their community who needed support and a sympathetic ear. Although the family had few resources themselves, they lived by a sort of code where it was always necessary to have extra food to feed guests. If somebody had a need, you would have to have a really good reason not to fill it. Anthony realized as he got older what a huge commitment his family made to be that open and available.

Anthony went to Catholic seminary at a young age and later became a monk. But something made him leave the monastery and go into the secular world; that transition seemed to have driven him to strive for success and excellence. It sounded like the structure of the monastic life helped him maintain an energetic balance; its fellowship supported him and its restrictions allowed him to avoid the stressful demands on his time, energy, and resources that he would face when he became a lay person.

The stories that Anthony told about his life all seemed to come back to this same theme; finding a balance between caring for others and being cared for, even by himself. He told stories about his first adult romantic relationships and the struggle to learn how to accept financial support. From his longtime volunteering in hospice programs, he told of a woman whose stubborn clinging to independence made it almost impossible to care for her. He told of caring for a young man who was incoherent due to having AIDS, and how he would have moments of lucidity that made Anthony feel like he was being blessed by the patient as a holy man might.

When we met, Anthony was in late middle age, in a long-term committed relationship, and was structuring his new job to create more flexibility for himself. That included progressively scaling back his work hours as he looks toward retirement and spending more of his resources on financial giving and volunteer work.

Part of staying in balance is seeing things realistically. We have little control over the world; however, we can affect our own experience and choices. Remembering this helps us to stay on track with our support and not become burned out or jaded. We have to really see the problems and barriers to change—those discussed in chapter 5 and others we discover. We have to understand that we are only a part of an effort to make change with a given problem. Most of us are not saints or saviors; we are people not unlike those we are trying to help. That is an important and difficult balance to hold. You care about this cause and have a passion to make it change for the better; at the same time, you can probably see how hard it is to create change because people have tried to make a difference for ages. If you can be optimistic as well as realistic, taking care of yourself in the process, it will be easier to be grateful for being in a position to help. That will help you to stay motivated and do what you can.

> The most important thing is the intention behind your giving and receiving. The intention should always be to create happiness for the giver and the receiver, because happiness is life-supporting and life-sustaining.
>
> Deepak Chopra and
> David Simon

It is difficult to navigate the line between favoring ourselves and caring for others, financially and otherwise. We all have needs and desires. Many of us have worked hard to distinguish our basic needs and understand what keeps us healthy and happy beyond those. Part of the resources we might contribute to the world we inherited, including our bodies and our spirits. Many religious traditions consider our physical body sacred, a gift from the cosmos or the divine. We might think of our bodies and spirits as precious instruments to use to benefit the world. This perspective helps us sustain our bodies and spirits so that we can continue to give and develop our capacity. Directing our energy both inward and outward is a complex balance that requires discernment, flexibility, and practices to which we can return.

Sustaining ourselves and understanding our own desires is different from needing to be important or powerful in the world; those are ego-based needs. The point is not to diminish ourselves or our own worth. Different people have different thresholds for what they are willing to sacrifice for the sake of making the world, or another's life, better. It is important not to judge by comparison. However, it is important to challenge yourself in this regard—to expand your concepts of what it is possible for you to do, to push an edge and see if that is too far for you.

Anthony recalled a time when he was with a small group of men at a weekend retreat. One of the men was just coming to terms with having been abused as a child. Anthony held him as his memories and grief surfaced; the man was even reacting physically by retching. Instead of feeling drained by the comfort he was giving, he recalls being able to hold his own equanimity, as if Anthony himself was also well taken care of in those moments.

That experience helped Anthony come to a new understanding of himself as a giver, and a new sense of freedom that has spilled over into his entire life. He felt more open to developing his spiritual life, so that it informed his deliberations about larger charitable donations, and planning his volunteer time. In those considerations, he found himself able to "hold both of these things: a very important need that I perceive, and my own need to not lose myself in taking care of others. It is not easy to hold that place, but it is a wonderful place that I never envisioned before."

Anthony also described how his financial giving evolved as he matured as an adult. When he was young, he had such a strong sense of responsibility that he did not feel like he had much choice—that he had to give until it hurt. In fact, he felt that not giving enough was a personal failure. Now he says, although that message is not entirely gone, he takes into account all of his giving, so in each instance he can moderate his efforts to keep them proportionate with what he has to give. He has also grown out of the idea that there were two distinct roles for him. In one, he was exclusively taking care of other people, which would take up most of his life. The other would happen eventually, when he could no longer help others and would have to accept support himself. Now he understands those roles as more fluid, with opportunities throughout life for both caring and being cared for. This is not only more reasonable; it has given Anthony more ease. He says, "Now I think of it as a flow that I do not have to monitor."

Resource Reckoning

If you are going to avoid some of the pitfalls listed in the previous chapter, you need to have a firm grasp on what your own resources are—materially as well as in skills, strengths, and experience. You will also need to consider your own needs and financial wherewithal. Some guidance for this is given at the end of this chapter in the Practices section. How do you structure your life and allocate your resources so that you can continue to grow in generosity over the next year, over the next decade, for your whole lifetime? How do you stay healthy, vibrant, and engaged? If you commit yourself to too much volunteer work; you will become exhausted and not able to do anything well. Similarly, if you do not have financial resources so that you and your family can live according to what you deem to be an appropriate level of well-being, it will be difficult for you to be open-handed and open-hearted. Discerning what level of generosity you can sustain without either hoarding or wasting money is personal and challenging. You might need to consider it over and over as your circumstances or views change. The only way to really know is to push it beyond your comfort zone and see if the new level works for you. If giving that much is sustainable, you may consider being even a bit more generous and then examine it again.

Consider the diagram on the following page about sustainability in generosity.

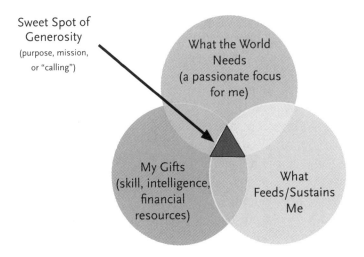

Spend some time thinking about your "sweet spot." If you can identify this area for your generosity work, it will feed you as much as you contribute to it!

This book focuses on you and your internal experience: your mission, your contributions, your challenges, your happiness, and your satisfaction. That is important because generosity emanates from your inner life, your behavior, and your actions. The quality of your internal state will affect how it manifests in the world around you. It can also keep you grounded in what is more deeply important to you. At the same time, being generous is about caring for other people, our planet, and its whole ecosystem. In stretching yourself, you might find that you are even more sensitive and empathetic to the plight of others and the organizations who struggle to make a difference.

If you want to be more generous, an essential step is to create a realistic (not fear—or fantasy-based) picture of what you and your family need to live today, and may need in the future. The practices at the end of this chapter will give some guidance in how to do this. It is my experience that most people do not formulate and try to live by a carefully crafted budget. Many people I encounter, although fully responsible and not living beyond their means, only account for their funds in the most general way and give themselves wide margins of cushion. If this is true for you, then clarifying exactly how much you are spending and on what will support your desire to be more giving, so you can set some goals for yourself. Then you can plan more accurately for the future. It will help to have a clear, written document of all of your current resources, including your insurance coverage and accounts toward retirement. Then you will also need an accurate accounting of your current monthly financial responsibilities and needs (expenses). The third part of this summary is what you are already giving as donations to people or organizations.

Although I would not be considered wealthy in the United States, I have a complex constellation of financial responsibilities, savings, investments, sources of income, insurances, and debts. If your situation is similar, consider seeing a professional financial planner. This person has been trained to consider an array of factors to help you make better plans.

When we endeavor to be more generous—by starting in our normal context and activities, allowing the necessary time and pacing, making and learning from our mistakes, after clearly and concretely accounting for all forms of our resources and resource needs—we can avoid risks. Over the longer term, these efforts can last and remain vibrant only by keeping to a scale that works in our life stage and maintaining the things that sustain us. For many of us, religious beliefs, community involvement, exposure to nature or the arts, and even our own memories help with these efforts.

PRACTICES

Financial Picture: Understanding Where You Are Today
Create a realistic financial picture that is sustainable and sufficient for yourself and your family, if you have one. This should include all of your income, savings, investments, property, and retirement benefits (resources). You will also need an accurate accounting of your

current monthly financial responsibilities and needs (expenses). This might already be captured in your monthly budget, or the great start of one. Next, summarize what you are already giving as donations to people or organizations—how much, how often, in what form, and to whom. When you put your resources, your expenses, and your current giving together, you should see an accurate picture of where you are today. This is one piece of the puzzle. We will put it together with your other considerations in later chapters.

Journaling

Give yourself permission to not be humble for a few minutes. No one else has your same combination of inherited qualities, your intelligence, knowledge from lessons you've learned, skills you have developed, your disposition, your social strengths, and perhaps even physical qualities. In your journal, make a list that is as complete as possible. Revisit it in a few days and see if you can refine or add to it.

Things that we find deeply meaningful will help to sustain us, even if they are not essential or part of our basic needs. As they fill one of the circles in the diagram above, you should identify them so you can engage them when they are needed. Take some time to be quiet and thoughtful. Once you are settled, list (or at least identify) one thing in your life that is deeply meaningful to you, not a basic need—something on which you spend time and/or money. This could be a hobby, a possession, an area of interest, an activity, or even a place you visit. In your journaling, address these questions:

- What about it fills you with joy, intrigues you, or always keeps you interested?
- How does it add richness to your life?
- How does it rejuvenate you, reconnect you with yourself, or "fill you up"?

It is important to sustain ourselves in ways we know are fulfilling. By focusing on this, we can be more mindful, choice-ful, and generous!

CHAPTER 7

Communities of Generosity

If you want to accelerate your practice of giving and receiving, join the kinship of a closely knit community. A community can leverage collective energies, resources, and intelligence at a much larger scale than individuals, so the group can effect social change or service projects in more potent ways. And communities can help grow the kind of world they imagine, according to their values and beliefs, by enacting and living it.

If that community depends on support from the financial resources and efforts of its members (which it most likely will), it will need your contributions—so it will also provide a place to develop your generosity. In fact, if you want to cultivate your generosity, you cannot find a better opportunity to do so than being active in an interconnected community. However, many communities miss the opportunity to support their members in developing their intentional generosity. Some communities actually thwart the giving of their members or act in ways that do not match their stated values—although they often do this inadvertently or out of frustration. If this is the case in a community where you find fellowship and shared purpose, you can help shift that and make the community more sustainable and congruent. This chapter aims to help develop your potential as a giver to your community. It might spark your ideas about how you can help change an element that may be impeding the generosity of your fellow community members.

For the purposes of this book, the term *community* is not geographic; it means a defined group of people in fellowship. For many people, this will mean their religious community—a church, synagogue, temple, or other gathering place. It could include a family community, but not all biological families form functional or charitable communities. Some fee-based and profit-oriented ventures, such as health clubs, can build community within its customer groups, however this rarely engages the whole membership or inspires a deep level of commitment. Not-for-profit organizations, meanwhile, rely mainly on their members to provide voluntary support, so community-building is more pivotal to achieving their goals.

If you are not an active member of any community, you may want to explore and visit social groups. Finding a community is not always easy, depending on your particular circumstances, yet is well worth the effort. If you seek a community, first look around to see if there are any people you already know with whom you share beliefs, activities, or interests and ask if they belong to a community you might join. Although you may find it difficult to identify the right community, you will be successful if you are open-minded, curious, and flexible.

Community Norms

Nonprofit communities usually have norms and shared values to which they ask their members to ascribe, related to giving time and/or financial resources, so you might consider the expectations of your own community. These norms can be stated overtly, which is common in some religious communities—usually undergirded by a specific faith or set of values. Tithing, which is discussed below, is one example. A practice such as tithing can present a beautiful challenge for some people, calling them into areas of growth they might never initiate themselves. For others, norms such as this are too restrictive and rigid; they do not accommodate for individual situations and development.

All the major religious traditions have something to say about giving of one's resources; each supports its own belief system and cultural context. It would take a whole book to explore them all. For this book's purposes, religious ideas about giving will be referenced in a limited fashion to give examples of their community-building aspects.

Nonreligious nonprofits also work to delineate norms in giving. For instance, if you serve on a nonprofit board, there may be a specific, written expectation for financial giving or for volunteering time to that organization. This may also have been true for Amy-Lee's (p. 108) parents, who were part of starting a Chinese school. Language and culture schools like this one are common in Asian-ethnic communities. Although some of them are sponsored by churches or other religious organizations, all parents are expected to give a significant amount of time and money to make the school happen.

Yet sometimes, communities do not directly, clearly, or generally make available their guidelines for giving behavior. Members must glean them from the community's stated values, or learn them by trial and error when participating in community activities. In this situation, participants can exercise personal discernment to find out what level of giving is right for them. My own congregation does not specify an expected amount for volunteering or charitable contributions.

> In the human world, abundance does not happen automatically. It is created when we have the sense to choose community, to come together to celebrate and share our common story.
> Parker J. Palmer

Communities such as this, with more loosely defined expectations, can allow for more individual behavior and can be more welcoming to people from diverse backgrounds. This welcoming may be especially appealing to those who seek communities with less restrictive responsibilities than they have experienced in the past.

However, some people find communities without specific guidelines to be confusing, and that can lead to misunderstandings or discomfort. Many congregations give little direct guidance for giving, leaving their members to wonder, sometimes for years into their participation, whether they are giving at appropriate levels.

Threefold Purpose

Many nonprofits have two tasks, aside from the effective management of their organizations: accomplish their mission goals and engage and build community support for their purposes. Some examples of these organizations include a local nonprofit that runs sports programs for youth sports; religious communities, which assist in faith development and create fellowship; and local giving circles. A giving circle is a group of people—often sharing fellowship—who pool their financial and other resources so that they can share the work of research and decision-making about worthy causes in order to make larger charitable gifts to nonprofits. (This is different from a stakeholder's circle, which is described in chapter 8.)

Because of the dual purpose of mission work and community-building, these organizations facilitate collective endeavors and serve as a touchstone for the participants regarding their personal values and purposes. This brings to mind Barbara (p. 6), who, once she and her husband established themselves financially, provided volunteer leadership and money to help found a local Jewish community center. This is a social and cultural center, based around Jewish values, that is supported through charitable donations, chiefly from its members.

Amy-Lee also provides an example of aligning her personal service goals with the goals of her congregation. In her process of gaining clarity about her financial and time resources, she decided to plan in advance for both her charitable giving and her volunteer time. She made an every-Sunday commitment to volunteer at her church, in a program to educate low-income people from the surrounding community. About this, she said:

Because it is part of First Parish, I feel more sustained in that work. I am better able to make that connection between what I am doing and why I am doing it because there is that underlying spiritual basis behind the work. I want to do it more than I would otherwise. I put more into it; it has become a bigger priority because it is attached to First Parish.

In addition to fulfilling a mission and leveraging the fellowship of community, there is still a third purpose. All the types of organizations listed above—religious communities, localized nonprofits, giving circles, and probably others—have the potential to be active communities of practice around growing generosity. Based on the fundamentally social nature of human learning, the idea of communities of practice comes from the work of cognitive anthropologists Jean Lave and Etienne Wenger.[18] A community of practice is "a group of people who share a concern or a passion for something they do, and learn how to do it better as they interact regularly." This is situated learning—learning that takes place in the same context in which it is applied. Using these concepts, a church community like Amy-Lee's can build fellowship with opportunities for giving and receiving; support faith development and other activities; and provide a setting to practice generosity—through education, modeling behavior, providing a setting for engagement, and mentoring in generosity.

A community of practice is a great way to rely on the intelligence and energy of others as you grow yourself. The benefits of learning in a community setting are extensive. They include gaining help with challenges, having access to people with more or different experiences, getting feedback to build your confidence, and having a venue for meaningful participation. Amy-Lee talked about how participating in a peer community has supported her development as a giver:

First Parish is a way to check in to make sure that my priorities are in order. It is the center for that: a place for me to think about how I give my time and money along with how others are spending their time and money. So I have to contribute in these ways. It is not optional, even if things get really busy. I have gone from volunteering and giving out of a vague sense of guilt; over time, I have come to see it as an obligation.

The tradition of tithing sheds light on this topic. In ancient times, when the Israelites were still a nomadic people, they wanted to act out their beliefs that recognized the Earth and everything in it as belonging to Yahweh (God). To demonstrate this, each household began to give a tenth of their livestock herds to the local religious leaders. Later these tithes would also include produce from the agriculture that developed. Tithing also went from being a tradition of faith to a form of cultic tax, and then became fixed in law. In addition to recognizing Yahweh's sovereignty, and encouraging obedience to God, tithing created identification with Israel and the temple. In this way, tithing was an important element in establishing the institution of the Jewish religion. As with ancient tithing, when we give to our faith community (or giving circle or nonprofit community), we are manifesting and practicing our beliefs, participating in the community's fellowship, and fueling its mission—including the support of the institution itself. At the same time, tithing propels us into a regular practice of giving; this might generalize into giving in other realms of our lives. Quite literally, it presents an opportunity for each of to align our beliefs, loves, and values with our financial and volunteer-time resources.

Developing Generosity in a Community Setting

Financial generosity in a closely knit community has rich benefits, but it can also present difficulties. In order to create and participate in an effective community of practice, it is crucial to embark on intentional giving yourself and understand how to encourage development in others. Yet in a community setting, it is also vital to avoid aspects that may harm the caring nature of the fellowship or misalign with the values of the community. Your participation in your community can help inform these practices so that the community welcomes its members' contributions.

A community of practice centered around generosity is not like an exchange relationship, where you give to and receive from the same person in like measure. Rather, you may give support to one person or part of the community, and receive support from another part. Giving in a community setting allows for a host of benefits. It can help create social acceptance, promote maturity, and challenge its members to give in "right relationship." It can also be a conduit through which one learns, practices values or beliefs, and benefits from the examples of other people. The experience can be a philanthropic kinship.

When you allocate your money and time to a community, this serves as a move toward deeper engagement and membership; you are putting "skin in the game." Contributing allows you to become part of your community in a way that you weren't before. Studies show that giving to a charitable organization facilitates the development of social relationships, because most charitable donations are made by people who are directly connected to the receiving organization or its beneficiaries.[19]

Over time, you may start to feel ownership for the organization and become what is sometimes called a steward. Amy-Lee expresses this experience from a contributor's perspective:

When I give money in an intentional way [to First Parish], it brings me closer, which I have never experienced before. It makes me care more, feel invested and that changes my relationship to that place. It goes beyond being a line item in my budget; it becomes an instrument of my engagement. I really try to think about what my relationship is and what I want to put into it. The money weirdly draws me into that conversation in a way that I might not otherwise have participated.

Amy-Lee also said that this more thoughtful and mature way of contributing helps her feel empowered and signifies for her that she is establishing herself as an adult. Younger people rarely have a dependable budget out of which to make charitable plans. Beyond that, it is helping her, in her own words, "to become a better person."

A community can also inform someone about how to live out its shared values through financial contributions. This is how Amy-Lee expresses her consideration of her beliefs and values when determining what her giving might be:

> When I joined First Parish a couple of years ago, it became the next way to figure out what my moral obligations are, related to what I can give. I had a completely secular upbringing, as my parents are atheists; we never went to or gave to a church, so I have no context to refer back to. I think religion and Unitarianism is a way for me to think through this; it has helped for me to push against something and it has worked. Seeing how things work at First Parish, and talking to other Unitarians about what compels them, helps as well.

As Amy-Lee points out, these communities also provide a way to observe the example of other people and how they are using their resources. These need not be explicit or structured mentorships. I have had this experience; in fact, I remember another member of my community saying to me, "I have pledged to do whatever I am asked to do whenever I am asked to do it, if I am able." That short statement challenged me because it is unequivocal in its generosity. Although that approach could lead to burnout if not exercised in moderation, it, along with the respect I have for that person, caused me to rethink my own willingness to give. Daniel (p. 70) was once a financially prosperous church member with no time to help in any way, and now he volunteers as the full-time building maintenance person. Adults and children who see his commitment to a life of service in their midst must be inspired.

When you are a member of a community that relies on its members for resources, you are often asked to contribute—and this greatly benefits a generosity practice. The community will ask you to contribute, either at a specific giving level or at a scale that befits your engagement and investment in the mission. One might call this aligning of your contributions, the giving amount, with the importance of the organization to you as being in *right relationship*. This task probably will require significant consideration and discernment, which will benefit you in associating your resources with your values.

This understanding of contributing turns fund-raising and volunteer recruitment on its head. It moves it from being a dreadful chore that few people want to do, and that makes the people being approached uncomfortable, to a consistent encouragement to be more generous and to consider the best use of one's resources. Asking people for money or to volunteer supports them in building closer relationships, creating greater meaning in their lives, and realizing their personal missions. What better place to act upon this than in a caring fellowship, where everyone is committed to its values and purpose? Amy-Lee said, "Because I am part of that community, I would not feel right walking in if I did not feel like every part of my life was moving toward the dreams we share in that place, that everyone gets behind."

Challenges to Community Building and Generosity

Picture your own community, or imagine one. It is a set group of people. Members may come and go, yet there is always a dedicated corps of participants. They help to create activities and programs for the community according to its values, volunteer to make
text continues on page 110

AMY-LEE

The congregation is a place to keep my priorities in order, to think about how I give my time and money, and learn from others.

—Amy-Lee

As a successful writer, Amy-Lee gives language easily to her ideas and concepts. She has a gentle demeanor, yet she is obviously ambitious—and very mature for a young adult. As a first-generation Chinese American, Amy-Lee seems to still be integrating the culture of her parents with the values and context of an urban, modern American life. Her talk is frank and passionate; she often draws her hand to her heart when describing her challenges. Despite the distractions that surrounded us in the busy coffee shop where we met, she held her focus and seldom looked away, except when deep in thought, and her eyes regularly sparkled with intense engagement.

Amy-Lee's parents left China for Midwestern America after having been active, while carrying a tiny Amy-Lee, in the Tiananmen Square protests in the late 1980s. Once settling in the United States, they continued their political activism, discussing issues with their children, and became key volunteers in creating and running a Chinese school. These schools are an established part of the Chinese immigrant community; through these, their culture, language, and beliefs pass on to the next generation. Her parents helped found the school where she attended, dedicated a huge amount of their time and money to build the school, and served as leaders long after Amy-Lee aged out. Although there was some religious teaching in the school, as local pastors were involved, Amy-Lee's parents were atheists who never belonged or contributed to a church.

When we met, Amy-Lee had been attending a Unitarian Universalist congregation and was serving as a volunteer leader in a social-justice program. She came to that church because of its history of social change leadership, not expecting to be drawn into the more religious aspects of membership nor the benefits of fellowship there. Her congregation creates a context for her justice work and informs her values, provides her with models, and is a place where she can focus her giving. For the first time, she also did some personal financial planning, informed by her congregational involvement, which allowed her to be more intentional and generous with her financial contributions.

The most remarkable thing about Amy-Lee was the passion and intensity she brought to her own consideration of connecting her values with her resources. Through budgeting and financial planning, she was looking deeply into the lifestyle she wanted create with her resources—how much consumption, how large a home and in what neighborhood, how much charitable giving would fit with her strong belief in investing in social change. Although she did not make any direct connections between her parents' charitable and justice efforts, and her current engagement with her religious community, one might easily deduce how one led naturally to the other.

---

them happen, and contribute financially. For new people entering this community, and for people who are changing their level of engagement from participant to member, or member to leader, it is natural for them to try to align their behaviors with others in the community. If you are part of a dedicated community, you may understand this, or you may have experienced it yourself. You join an organization, and immediately you want to know what you are expected to contribute. Your first question is probably, "What are other people giving?" Amy-Lee asks this precise question:

> Once I am done with my financial planning, I wonder— what do other people give and how do they make those decisions? That is a challenge: What percentage might I donate to First Parish, and how does that fit with other people's giving? I still don't know how to figure that out.

These comparisons to other people may help provide guidance about appropriate giving levels, but they also present an inherent problem. Each person has a different set of resources, understands the use of those resources in a distinct way, and has a different level of engagement and investment in the organization. Also in the financial realm, the aspects of their economic life—their debts, responsibilities, potential income, savings, investments— are entirely unique, so their capability is also unlike anyone else's. A paltry financial commitment to you may be a crushing burden to someone else. A painful stretch gift for you may be almost unnoticeable to another person. Usually, these financial factors are unknown to even our most intimate friends. So the comparison-based guidance is only helpful in a general way and does not provide much help with either making decisions about giving or growing a generosity practice.

Unfortunately, what usually follows on the heels of comparing is judgment. Part of the purpose of social comparisons is the attempt to craft accurate self-evaluations: How am I doing? To do this, one must engage in evaluating other people. This is neither a moral failure nor a sign of poor character; it is a natural phenomenon of human interaction. But in deciding what to do with these evaluations, we can make a choice about our social comparisons. Amy-Lee was open about this challenge:

> Although I don't know how they think about these things, I assume a lot of my friends do not think of money this way [as a way to create meaning, support social justice, and increase belonging]. I would guess that they think of it as—I want to spend money on different things I want. I am trying not to judge, but it does seem that people aren't distinguishing needs from wants. My next-door neighbor from childhood is getting married and has asked for cash as a wedding present. She does not need the money, and I would rather give to a cause in her name instead. I do not know if that is right, if I am imposing my ideas on her. It is kind of confusing.

Any comparison or judgment about other people's giving only hampers the formation and maintenance of community bonds. These barriers to deeper social connection may personally affect you. This is also true of making assumptions about other people's resources. When comparison, judgments, or assumptions are expressed verbally or in written materials, they actually inhibit generosity in the larger community. This approach spreads fear of judgment. When people sense that they are being evaluated, they hold back their contributions of time and money. This is the opposite of a welcoming invitation to be generous.

Some groups make comparisons to the giving in other communities. For instance, a religious organization may gather data comparing their average giving levels to those of other denominations or local nonprofits, and then use the data to demonstrate to donors that they could be giving more. This does a disservice to the other denominations or nonprofits, as their missions and belief systems are entirely different. The context for giving is dissimilar. And this kind of comparison can be experienced by donors as a form of disguised judgment about the scale of their gifts.

Another concern about community-based giving relates to the openness of the community to people from economically diverse backgrounds, or to people who have differing amounts of time to volunteer. If the community holds rigid expectations for giving, if it encourages comparison, then people who have less to give may find themselves less welcome, and people with more to give may be given positions of status. This creates a stratified community, which inhibits true fellowship. It also encourages thinking according to an exchange relationship: For everything you give to the community in whatever form, you expect something of like value in return. However, most communities provide benefits, such as caring, that do not lend themselves to a tit-for-tat system. And for the community to sustain itself, people who have more to give usually need to give more to compensate for people who cannot give as much.

> Generosity is not only an individual virtue that contributes to human well-being, but that it is an openness to others that is fundamental to human existence, sociality, and social formation.
>
> Rosalyn Diprose

Sometimes, people are concerned that donating to help support the development of the organization rather than its service or programs might just be insulating the community—"feather-nesting"—to make the community more comfortable or esthetically pleasing for its members. This seems to be the opposite of implementing a social mission and working for the betterment of the larger society.

This is a complex question. Most nonprofits or religious communities are open to anyone. Typically, their programs and activities are accessible to all, with the only conditions that participants refrain from extreme behavior, share common interests, ascribe to their values, and/or hold the same set of beliefs. Many organizations have programs for welcoming and look for new participants, so even the conditions of shared interests, beliefs, and values are suspended for newer people. This is often part of the core mission of the organization. Part of this welcoming is to maintain the structure people enter into, be it a website or a building, so the community is hospitable and functions well. To create and maintain these welcoming conditions, and provide unpaid entry to the community, the community needs member contributions. Building and maintaining a place to grow relationships engenders kinship. We need to practice living together in diverse communities in order to build kinship with those we hope to benefit.

For Amy-Lee, and for others, this presents tension because she is one of the beneficiaries of the mission of her home congregation. She not only fuels the organization through her generosity, she is also receives that generosity. She said,

> I don't know what to do about giving to First Parish versus other causes and organizations; it feels like apples to oranges. First Parish is a place where I feel that I benefit directly, so that inclines me to give more to other organizations, which is a bit backwards. The more I give to First Parish, which is a place that helps other people to think about this topic [charitable giving], that seems like it might make a bigger difference.

In my congregation, higher giving levels do not provide me greater status or benefits. It is an anti-status culture that promotes social equality for all. I do not get a better seat at events, more access to support, or have more power to influence pivotal decisions because I give money at a certain level. No matter what level of donation I give, my congregation will provide its benefits to me in full measure, the same as anyone else. This creates an opening for people from across the full economic spectrum, including those with limited resources and high-net-worth individuals. Naturally, if I volunteer at leadership levels in the organization, I will have greater influence on its workings; yet this must be held within the agreements and structures endowed by the community itself, and not for personal gain.

When status and power are diffused in this way, everyone feels invited to step forward with their resources. For instance, let's say you are a holder of great wealth. In this fellowship, you want to belong; you want to be known and cherished for the totality of your being as the basis of your relationships there. Therefore, you do not want to be separated from the rest of the fellowship because of your level of giving. This belonging creates the conditions for you to give generously according to your capacity. The same is true if you have limited financial resources. You want to be appreciated for all of who you are, and honored for the resources you contribute within your personal capacity to give.

When what you gain is separated in this way from how much you give, it allows you to take your own self-interest out of the calculus, leading you to the consideration of right relationship. In this way, your community serves as a polished mirror, calling you to accurately reflect on your own values and resources. Your community prompts you to give in ways that fuel your own growth in generosity rather than improving your level of status.

Inviting Generosity

Think about the aspects of community life that engage your generosity. The best way to cultivate giving is to involve all the members in a community of practice around generosity; to help all community members discern right relationship in giving through guidance, education, and modeling. Engaging as many people as possible, in whatever resource drives or campaign processes are needed, creates this alignment and disproves the belief that it is an unpleasant yet necessary aspect of community life. Instead, the organization and its members can understand generosity as at the core of their mission and a way to build not only organizational sustainability, but fellowship between members.

In order to be truly welcoming to new people, a community must be as explicit as possible about the expectations of membership —including levels of financial giving for people with various resource levels—yet without being overly prescriptive. Most people want to know what "the deal is" before formally joining a group. It also helps to allay any suspicions about hidden expectations, norms, or "fees." Also, if people who have been involved for some time have a shared understanding of the expected level of giving, and this is not openly communicated with newcomers, it creates the impression of an insider's group. Communities with insiders must also have outsiders. New people naturally assume they are part of the latter category. This could make them feel unwelcome.

Communities can give their members the greatest opportunities to practice generosity. They can let people know that generous giving will increase their feeling of belonging and join them in fellowship. Whether the norms are clearly stated or are loose expectations, they can communicate that participants' own circumstances and relationships to the organization should help determine actual giving levels. Communities can make sure their systems accommodate a broad range of giving capability, neither shaming people with deep pockets nor embarrassing people with tight finances. Also, they should state their expectations clearly, using a sliding scale or form that allows people to determine their own level of giving. This goes beyond a percentage of income, a one-size-fits-all solution, because our financial lives are too complex for simple formulae.

The organization should inspire people with its mission and vision; its purpose should be compelling to its members. Some people will also need clear and explicit information about the finances and systems of the organization. It should provide that data in an accessible, usable format.

The organization also can share the stories of boldly generous members, as well as the benefits they experience. This can be done in multiple forms and through any communication vehicle.

The community also should communicate that giving to support the community itself is important. The community stands at the center of the mission and serves as a launching pad for most of its mission activities. As the tithe actually helped to solidify and institutionalize the Jewish community, so your giving to your own community—be it a nonprofit, giving circle, or religious community—helps it to become more established, secure, and enduring.

About Anonymity

Some givers want their identity withheld when they give a financial gift. Normally, organizations will honor this request. Many think that making anonymous gifts is the most selfless and humble way to contribute. Some religious traditions reinforce the notion of anonymous gifts, and nonprofits offer this option to all of their donors.

The Jewish scholar and philosopher Maimonides proposed a "Ladder of Charity" in his famous treatise, *The Guide of the Perplexed.*[20] This eight-rung ladder defines degrees of virtue in the giver. The first and lowest rung is the type of giving done begrudgingly; it makes the recipient feel disgraced or embarrassed. The eighth and highest rung creates the most opportunity for the beneficiary to become fully independent and so is considered a higher form of approach to giving than an outright gift, which can induce shame in the recipient. An example of eighth-rung giving includes providing an interest-free loan or entering a business partnership with someone in need of charitable gifts. Rungs five, six, and seven have to do with the revealing of identity, or anonymity. At level five, the giver does not know to whom they are giving, yet the receiver knows the identity of the giver. At level six, the recipient does not know who gave the gift, yet the giver knows who the recipient is. At level seven, neither the giver nor the recipient knows the other's identity. Here, the condition of anonymity is supposed to reduce ego-driven gifts by the giver and promote respect for the person needing resources. In this system, anonymity is portrayed as more virtuous.

Barbara told a story of participating in a holiday present drive for financially strapped families; it illustrates a potential pitfall of building donor anonymity into a program. Although Barbara's family members are practicing Jews, the whole extended family bought Christmas presents for a family that otherwise would not have them. They arranged this through a local nonprofit, which gave them the genders and ages of all of the family's members. Barbara's family shopped all together, including the children, who were especially excited to pick out things these other kids would like. They wrapped the presents together and went to drop them off. When they arrived with the presents, they were told that they would not be able to give them directly, nor have the family's contact information. Although this may have been intended to protect the beneficiary family in some way, it disappointed Barbara and her family. She said, "We were careful about picking out just the right gifts and wanted to see their excitement about them. It was not like we wanted a reward, but it seemed disconnected and disappointing. We never did that again."

Although it is unfortunate that Barbara and her family did not get to meet and possibly build friendships with the family that received their gifts, she handles the disparities with a group of female friends well. These women friends are close and see each other often. Some of them work as teachers or social workers, professions that require great knowledge and skill compared with their financial compensation. Barbara's husband is a successful lawyer. Aware of the financial inequity, yet valuing the work of her friends, Barbara often pays for their meals when they go out. She said, "I just feel that by me picking up the tab, I even things out a little. And that way, they don't feel uncomfortable. I try to make the money part unimportant when we are together, so we can stay close." This is an expression of her care and respect for her friends, and it helps to bind them together as a community. It also may make it possible for them to participate; it breaks down an economic divide in a equality-oriented way. Finally, Barbara talks to them about it and separates their level of wealth from the value of their contributions to society. This honors them and may make them feel noble in their professions. Barbara, by being overt and visible with her gifts, is able to create positive effects that she could not do with an anonymous gift. This story illustrates a way to talk about money and giving that nurtures everyone.

Although Barbara did not reference Maimonides, she expressed her preference for anonymity with her larger gifts: "I never wanted to be treated differently because we gave." Yet her two stories illustrate how anonymity can present significant limitations to growing one's own generosity and supporting others on their paths. With these lesser acts of generosity, Barbara speaks for herself and navigates the challenges of disparate resources openly. Speaking about yourself in an open, frank, and, most of all, caring way engages people. People really do want to talk about money and giving, yet are concerned about navigating the issues of privacy and status and the lack of clarity that usually results.

When you talk about giving money, it is as if you are standing a little farther along a path, calling back to tell people how you are finding your way. You are not telling them where to go, for they have their own path. Instead, you can reveal that you are on a journey as well, and you do not have all of the answers for yourself either. You can talk about how you find your way: You think about it, gather information, discern, plan, and implement. Of course, for this to be effective, you have to first be giving and set a positive example for people to follow. It does not assume their level of inspiration, commitment, or capability to give. And it does not hamper their generosity by defining its form or quantity.

Considering Gifts to Core Community

If you or other community members are inviting newcomers and providing guidance to make contributions to the community, a gracious and nonjudgmental approach will be the most effective. This is important enough to bear repeating: Being financially generous runs counter to mainstream consumer culture. Many people have not made the connections that Amy-Lee and others interviewed for this book have made. To be truly generous is a great challenge that requires personal dedication to the practice. Not everyone has the capacity or "calling" to do it. To effectively encourage others, community members should meet people where they are, while being inspiring and crafting a caring invitation.

My own community of practice happens to be a Unitarian Universalist congregation. My experience may be useful when considering the scale of giving to causes and organizations you care about. I consider myself central to my congregation, and more peripheral to the other organizations to which I contribute regularly. I say this because there is essentially only one group of donors to my core community, and those are the members like me. We are also the main volunteer corps, and we have a lot of say about what we do (program and mission activities), how we do it (according to our

> If you have come here to help me, you are wasting your time. . . . But if you have come because your liberation is bound up with mine, then let us work together.
> Lilla Watson

values), and who we hire to serve as core staff members, supporting these efforts. Perhaps just as important, as I am an active and engaged part of my community; if I removed myself, I would leave a gap that people would notice. With other nonprofits, although I financially support their purposes and activities, and sometimes volunteer as well, I am not central to their efforts. I am one of many contributors, which may include foundations and government programs as well as individuals. I have no role in how those other organizations are run, how they define their values, the strategies they use, or who they engage to make their mission activities happen. If I decided to withdraw my support, although it may be noted in their database, I would not really be missed.

Part of my decision about giving to my congregation relates to honoring the people and events that have established it and furthered the mission before me. My giving also helps to ensure that the congregation is there long after I am gone, for people I will never meet and children who have yet to be born. Between honoring the past and preparing for the future, my gifts warrant the vitality of the programs and activities we implement today—which accord intimately with my own values. In this way, my congregation creates a broader vehicle for making a difference in the world than I could make myself.

Finally, as you might expect, my congregation is my community of practice. It is a central venue for my generosity practice, and there I am determined to develop my ability to receive and give—with my financial resources, time, intelligence, muscle, and skills. In the process, I also try to be an inspiring voice, inviting people to join me in developing generosity, thereby furthering our collective goals.

PRACTICES

Generosity Interviews

Among your acquaintances, who would consider very generous? Some of them may have come to mind as you were reading. Contact one or two of them and ask if you could interview them. Meet wherever it is convenient for both of you; plan to spend about forty minutes for each interview. Once you get into it, you may take longer! On the next page, you will find questions for the interview—essentially the same ones used for the interviews included in this book.

Journaling

Reflect on what you learned in the generosity interviews:

- How were their experiences different from your own, or those in this book?
- What did that teach you about generosity and how it works?
- Did this conversation create a closer connection with the person you interviewed?
- What possibilities did the interview open up for your own practice or community?

Next, take a few minutes to reflect on your own social network (at work, family, community/activity groups, or spiritual community). If you wish, draw a map with yourself in the center, and your connections to groups around the center. Try to envision your ideal network. Consider:

- Are there connections you want to make stronger?
- Are there connections that you used to have that are missing?
- Are there connections that tax your time or resources and that are not fulfilling for you?
- How can you use your gifts and openness to receiving to build the ideal network for yourself?
- What is the first step you will take in that direction, and when?

Interview Questions for Generous People

1. Learning About Generosity
   a. What is your first memory of charitable giving to someone else?
   b. What did you learn in your childhood about sharing or not sharing your resources?
   c. How did you learn that and from whom?
   d. Was there someone who was a role model or mentor for you around being financially generous?
   e. Can you point to a time in your life where your attitudes or actions with being financially generous had a marked change?
      i. What led to that change?

2. Receiving Generosity
   a. Have you ever been on the receiving end of someone else's generosity?
   b. What was that like for you?
   c. Has receiving caused you to change to how you think about giving to others?
   d. If you had to, could you rely on someone else's generosity?

3. Generosity and Values
   a. Why do you feel it important to be generous?
   b. How does your generosity relate to your ethics, beliefs, or spiritual life?
   c. What supports your generosity? If you cannot identify any, what kind of support might you like?

4. Internal Benefits of Generosity
   a. When you give charitably, what has been your internal experience? What thoughts, feelings, or ideas have you had?

    b. Have you been able to help someone else in an important way? What was that like?

    c. Is *your* life different in any way as a result of your giving efforts?

5. Barriers to Generosity
    a. What are the greatest barriers to you being generous?
    b. When you think about ways that you would like to be more generous, what prevents you from doing that?

6. Giving in a Community Setting
    a. Do you belong to a community where giving is encouraged, taught, or modeled?
    b. Has your family ever been involved in giving as a group effort?
    c. What are the benefits of giving together rather than independently?

7. Teaching Generosity
    a. If you wanted to guide someone to be more generous, how would you go about doing that?
    b. Which pieces would you be sure to include?

CHAPTER 8

Giving Skillfully

Giving generously is also giving skillfully and with a strategy—as a philanthropist. As Elise (p. 56) comments, "I realize that sometimes I give just because I want it off my desk. Real generosity is giving knowledgeably and consciously and intentionally, with purpose. Not because some organization contacts me." The aim of this chapter is to give you information and tools to follow Elise's direction. It provides general information you might need when assessing nonprofits before you give them donations; it discusses their systems, which you will encounter as a financial donor, and includes information on forms and strategies for you to consider in your giving.

A nonprofit is an organization that, rather than distributing surplus revenues as profit or dividends, uses them for its self-preservation, expansion, or programs—to achieve its mission goals. Although these organizations are not the only outlet for your charitable gifts, people most commonly give their money to nonprofits, so much of this information will cover how they function in regard to donors like yourself.

Most nonprofits seek and have a 501(c)(3) tax-exempt status designation from the Internal Revenue Service (IRS). This exempts the organization from income tax and other taxes. With this designation, your financial donations to that organization may be used as deductions against your income when filing your taxes. Nonprofits range in size and funding from small and resource-challenged to large and well-funded. For instance, Harvard University is a charitable organization according to the IRS; it has the largest university endowment in the world at about $30 billion in 2012.

Many nonprofits have well-developed, sophisticated fundraising systems. Once you have made a donation, you will almost certainly receive further communication from them. When you, as a donor, look at these organizations through a lens of developing generosity, you will see systemic problems. You may be able to deal with them by understanding these issues, looking for ways to counter them, seeking deeper benefits in the process, and doing some investigation into the organizations—so you are assured of the best use of your gifts.

Once upon a time, fundraising in the nonprofit sphere was a simple matter, done with substantial creativity by non-professionals trying to support a specific mission. Self-sustaining communities still largely leverage the efforts of volunteers to raise the money they need. However, now in the nonprofit world there are undergraduate and even graduate degrees in fundraising, as well as well-developed specialty areas, consultancies, and reams of research on the topic. This chapter provides general information tailored to what you might need to know to be a skillful donor. If you want more information, consult fundraising resources at your local library or online.

Nonprofits gain their financial fuel through a few broad categories of sources. These include earned income from programs or services they provide, government funding, private funding from foundations and corporations, and individual donors.

To reach individual donors like you, nonprofit fundraising programs purchase lists and have paid staff or contractors who make generalized solicitations. These are done though virtually every medium: postal mail, phone, and the Internet. Non-professional supporters also engage and recruit people they know, either by postal mail, on the web, or by going door-to-door. Some nonprofits raise revenue by selling products unrelated to their mission. Examples include schools sending their students out to sell wrapping paper or chocolate, and the Girl Scouts selling cookies. Fundraising events also are used to draw new donors; they come in many forms: 5K walk-a-thons, auctions, receptions, parties, and asking directly for donations at in-person meetings. Each of these types of approach have a different expense ratio for the nonprofit. Usually the least expense comes from asking directly at a meeting. The greatest expenses come from large events where the giving level is low, like a sporting event or auction. In those instances, when you as a donor receive a salable product or service as part of the donation process, the amount of the actual donation is reduced— as is the amount that is potentially tax deductible. In self-sustaining communities, members most commonly solicit each other, usually with the only incentive being the benefits to the community itself and its mission purposes.

> The one who controls himself and controls his life can be truly generous, and give without effort, expecting nothing and asking for nothing but his strength to give and to work.
>
> Albert Camus

Using exchange relationships is common among nonprofits— in which you are given items as incentives to prompt a charitable gift. Yet using the exchange of goods or benefits for donations may actually limit the amount you may be willing to contribute. Research shows that receiving gifts in exchange for donations may inhibit some of the inherent or more altruistic motivations for giving. In some studies, people who received large gifts were more likely to donate smaller amounts, while those who received no gift were most likely to donate in larger amounts.[21] Another danger of offering benefits in exchange for donations is that they may confuse or offend potential donors. Some donors take offense at the organization spending their financial contributions on trinkets or expensive events in what they perceive as a wasteful way. British researchers Tom Farsides and Sally Hibbert note that donors may also think that the organization does not share the donor's altruistic goals. Donors may suspect that the organization is more concerned with meeting its fundraising targets, improving its standing, or wielding influence in its field than helping the beneficiary group, which is supposed to be its focus.[22]

Nonprofit organizations use databases to track their donors' information, donation history, and preferences. They are used for communications and to make well-targeted requests to donors like you, based on the available information. Nonprofits also use software that delivers information on the wealth of individuals, their other charitable donations, political affiliation, religious membership, the value of their property, and other personal information. Much of this information is in the public sphere and companies gather, package, and sell it for profit. These are rarely used in self-sustaining communities, where members not only know each other already, but are sensitive about their peers gathering information about them that they have not voluntarily disclosed.

There is a progression of donor engagement that usually correlates to the amount of the financial gifts to be solicited. The initial goals of fundraising programs are to attract new donors, who usually give smaller, one-time, or occasional donations. People who have more knowledge and involvement with the organization may then make regular or annual gifts. Donors who are even more loyal to the organization and its mission may set up regular gifts that continue until the donor halts them. A dedicated donor, at the next level, may make what is called a major gift (however that is defined by the organization), or a larger gift to a capital campaign.

If you are a donor at this level, you may be asked to join a donor's or stakeholder's circle. These are hosted by a single organization, such as a nonprofit or university, to cultivate high-amount donors. Because of this, the circle may be named according to the mission or identity of the host organization, for instance, a "Scholar's Circle." The host organization normally puts substantial time and effort into deepening the donor's knowledge about the organization and its mission area. Although the name is similar, this is quite different from a giving circle. As described in chapter 7, giving circle members are independent from any organization, often share fellowship, and make their own decisions about which charitable organizations will receive their pooled donations. Members in a stakeholder's circle relate directly to the host organization and do not usually pool their resources or participate in the designation of their donations.

If you are a highly dedicated donor, you may set up a gift through a legal instrument such as your will or a trust fund, or through designating the nonprofit in your insurance or invested funds. Such methods for planned giving are being developed all the time to suit situations particular to individual donors and their financial situations. As a donor, you should know that the goal of fundraising programs is to move you along this progression to ever-higher levels of giving. Donor progression occurs in self-sustaining communities as well, yet usually it happens more naturally; orchestrated attempts to actively move donors to higher levels are rare and must be done with a high level of sensitivity.

Political fundraising deserves a mention. These fundraising efforts are intense because their timelines are by definition limited (usually stopping on the day of the vote), while their scale and reach can be immense. They use all the techniques listed above and in addition leverage complex and sometimes opaque systems, such as political action committees (PACs) and super-PACs, that make it difficult for donors like you to do skillful diligence when considering a gift.

In these current systems, nonprofits compete for money. These programs must not only to be creative but aggressive to gain the income they need to meet their goals. Nonprofit staff members and volunteers are passionate and mission-driven people who are trying to be successful in their system. Donors like you are the logical players to take the lead on making changes so that you, organizational fundraisers, and even beneficiaries feel less pressure and can expend more resources on their mission ends.

Donor Benefits

Many donors exchange their donations for what are called donor benefits. Some material benefits you may gain as a donor are listed above. In addition to those, you may be recognized as a planned and legacy giver in the form of a plaque, paving stone, listing in a significant place, or some other way to assure that you will be remembered.

Yet some donor benefits are intangible. For instance, as a donor you might be invited to a social event or performance for your own enjoyment. You might be eligible to use support and fitness training, to get in shape or improve your own performance in an athletic event. After giving a larger amount of money, you may obtain volunteer roles that offer opportunities to exercise influence and decisions about how the organization is run. Or you may be honored in a public way, such as having something important named after you—an award, scholarship, room, or even a building. This may improve your public image or raise your status in the community.

Assuming that you and other donors are authentic in your intent to support the organization's mission, there is nothing morally wrong with this system. If the organization follows the logical progression of engagement, then the giver will learn more about the organization and have more opportunities to engage in their mission as they go along.

However, these systems do have downsides. First of all, these donor benefits cost the organization money. Nonprofits spend a lot to maintain this system and its fundraising staff. Figures are hard to come by because program costs often are not clearly divided from other expenses that the organizations incur. Some costs are also difficult to quantify, such as the cost of maintaining a donor memorial garden in perpetuity. Because nonprofit organizations are required to make information publicly available, there are sources that will tell you how much of an organization's budget goes to administrative and fundraising costs. Some of these sources are listed below. However, unless you are ready to do some deeper and more thorough investigation into the finances and functioning of the organization, this information alone will not be sufficient.

You might expect reports on exactly how the money you gave was spent—a description of the activities of the charitable organization and figures that illustrate what measurable change occurred. In recent years, donor demand has fueled a movement to more accurately measure nonprofits' activities, similar to what for-profit corporations can provide. However, these methods are sometimes not transferable due to differences in those two sectors. Sometimes, evaluation methods create data designed to appeal to donors, but that is not useful to the actual nonprofit. Foundations and larger individual donors sometimes require onerous and specific reporting requirements. This practice occurs in the name of improving the nonprofit's effectiveness, but it creates a disconnection from what is manageable and useful for the nonprofit involved and thus seems oriented to the donor's or foundation's own goals and purposes.

Higher-level donors sometimes wield a certain amount of power within the organization. They do this by targeting, or restricting, their gifts to certain programs and thereby expanding those parts of the organization, which in the extreme can cause mission drift—decisions that alter the course of the organization away from its stated mission. In many cases, high donors are asked to serve on the board or other important committees. This may be because they are well-informed and passionate about the mission and organization. Nonprofit executives also might hope that they will give more large gifts or ask their wealthy peers for donations. This can be an effective strategy, yet if the donor's role as a volunteer is unclear, it might create a platform for undue influence in matters beyond governance, such as staff evaluations or implementation strategies. Because nonprofit organizations cease to be viable without these donor dollars, and because money buys so much entitlement in our culture, it is difficult for these organizations to resist these influences. Unfortunately, sometimes they are based on personal passions or false opinions that are beyond the best interests of the organization's overall mission.

The more sophisticated and extensive the fundraising program is, and the more valuable the donor benefits, the more it costs the organization—in money, attention, human resources, and other ways. Those resources are dedicated to the sole purpose of engaging you in a way that you will give them some of your money, and not to address their core mission. Some donors demand that nonprofits hold these costs down, and may even withhold donations, but this just puts the nonprofit under pressure and can reduce their competitiveness for other donor dollars. There is another way to reduce these fundraising costs: to help people like you strengthen your connections to the mission activities of the organization and develop your practice as a generous donor.

Engaging the Beneficiaries

In some cases, one or more aspects of a nonprofit's fundraising campaign—the form, the language, the symbols, or something else—offends donors and/or beneficiaries, and the campaign fails, despite the success of the organization's mission programs. In most cases, this happens because the nonprofit's staff has not fully considered or understood the effects on donors and beneficiaries. As a donor, you want the organizations you support to perform at their best, not wasting resources on misaligned efforts or offending their constituents. This is especially true if you are dedicated to the organization and its mission. Nonprofits can avoid these mishaps by engaging with their beneficiaries and donors before launching fundraising programs.

In one case, a nonprofit that benefits people with autism started a public-awareness and fundraising campaign where they asked people from the general public to refrain from communicating through electronically based social media for a period of time. The messaging said that this would be in solidarity with those who have an autism diagnosis. The campaign drew strong reaction from the autism community because it implied that people with autism cannot communicate.[23] In fact, electronic communication is one of the ways many people with autism manage their condition. People in that community also value social media as a vehicle for educating the public about their experiences.

In another instance, an organization that supports people with Multiple Sclerosis (MS) and fights for a cure created a logo with the letters "MS" in a circle with a black line across it. Although this may have been intended to mean to depict a stamping out of the disease, one respondent felt that that it might also symbolize crossing out people with MS. That same organization put on a series of challenging bike rides and walks. Some people with MS are unable to participate in these events because of the effects of the disease, so they are left with a supporting role for people able to do those activities. This could serve as a sad reminder of what they have lost to the degenerative disease.[24]

There are many instances of donations that are wasted or that are inappropriate for the beneficiaries. It is also easy to find stories of donations that created unexpected consequences. In Africa, reforestation projects that cleared damaged trees have resulted in increased fire risk, soil degradation, and loss of wildlife. At one point, millions of Pop Tarts were airlifted and dropped into Afghanistan. Instead of providing nutrition or improving the image of America, many of these snacks ended up on the local black market.[25]

Of course, any giving can go awry; there is no guarantee that your giving will always be properly directed. Yet when you ensure that the beneficiaries are engaged in creating the solutions, it makes this more likely—and builds solidarity. As a donor, you can also ask nonprofits to give you information about how their programs, communications, and fundraising campaigns are created with substantive (not token) involvement of the people who are the intended beneficiaries. Naturally, the better your understanding of the beneficiary group or cause, the more able you will be to choose a nonprofit that addresses it well.

Uniting the Community of Concern

The challenges listed above result from an underlying structural dynamic wherein the donors, the nonprofit staff members and volunteers, and the beneficiaries are considered as discrete groups with separate levels of status. The most empowered of these is the donor group; they have the resources that nonprofits need, so they in turn are the ones to whom nonprofits frequently cater. The beneficiaries are the people with needs, who are clearly the best-informed about what they need, although they are often excluded from decision-making in the organization. In the middle are the staff members and volunteers, who are usually the best-informed about strategies to deliver programs, often have a broad view of the issues involved, and are the most attuned to the subtleties of the outcomes. These groups are often distinct, and in some cases they are intentionally kept separated.

This is a great loss. Traditional nonprofit structuring works against the potential for generosity to build kinship among these groups, or even blur the distinction between givers and receivers. It also creates a dynamic where the staff members and volunteers are pulled by donor demands in one direction and by beneficiary needs in the other—neither of which they can ignore. The beneficiary group is often larger or has a greater level of need than the staff and volunteers can address. This may be one of the causes of staff and volunteer burnout.

Who is in the best position to change some of these dynamics? Nonprofit boards and staff can institute policies to prevent these types of problems. However, donors—people like you—are the most empowered ones and can create the most positive changes. Here is a new role for you as a philanthropist!

Multiple opportunities arise when we reconceive this dynamic. We can assume that the donors, volunteers and staff, and beneficiaries are all passionate about the issue at hand and united in their concerns. As one community of concern, all groups might join together to address the issue in a more integrated way. For this to happen, we donors would need to voluntarily forgo the empowerment to which we are accustomed. In our financial support of nonprofits, donors are trying to meet deep needs. We should acknowledge that we are less expert than either the staff or recipients, and so we should refrain from using our status for undue influence. The beneficiary group also should realize that they themselves are also resourceful and have much to contribute to this shared enterprise. In this way, both donors and the beneficiaries have needs to be filled and contributions to make. The staff and volunteers then find themselves in the much more manageable position of facilitating and coordinating efforts, rather than mediating between two interested but disparate groups. In this more kinship-based structure, the donation is not an end point for any of the people involved. Instead, it is a beginning with the potential for building solidarity.

You might see this as a naïve or improbable, yet it is relatively easy for you to affect as a donor—at least on a small scale. Truly generous impulses will help avoid some problematic aspects all together. All you have to do, as the person giving the financial gift, is to give without needing to be "romanced" by the nonprofit's staff and volunteers. Then give your donations without expecting any personal benefit—material or immaterial—in return. Anthony (p. 90) reflected this approach when he said, "With regard to my contributions, I know that it takes money to run organizations whose missions I care about, and I want to help them as much as I can, so I give."

Consider refusing any benefits offered you, letting the person or organization know that you would like them to funnel those resources back into the mission work. That means no "free" tote bags, CDs, or parties with the socially elite; no special honoring on a garden paving stone, on a building, or at an event; no power or influence in exchange for your financial gift. These kinds of benefits absorb one's attention and actually distract from or decrease the experience of the deeper benefits of being more altruistic.

If you are committed to the cause, spend time in direct service of that issue, which may mean getting to know the beneficiaries on a

text continues on page 138

HENRY

If you have the ability to give, it is a gift and you have to use it wisely.

—Henry

Although Henry is not from the South, he has a genteel Southern gentleman's demeanor and seems gracious to everyone around him. In middle age, he has created a comfortable but not extravagant life for himself working with a foundation on health issues in the developing world.

He describes himself as having two families; he was first raised by his mother and stepfather in the Midwest until his mother passed away. Then he moved to the Northeast and lived with his father and stepmother. His father owned a restaurant, so the family worked there almost every day of the year. Still, their home served as a focal point in the neighborhood; there were always people over. His father was charitable in small amounts to many different organizations. Henry's father instilled in him at an early age the ethic of service to people who needed it. He mowed lawns and shoveled snow as a volunteer, and donated a lot of his time helping out at church and school. This lasted through his college years.

In college, Henry gave his first charitable donation to a political candidate who shared his values. At the time, he was working multiple jobs to get through college, but he found this donation satisfying. It allowed him to have a larger voice, access to new worlds, and some influence. He now gives away a high percentage of his income, both formally to organizations and to individuals he knows who are in need. This use of money to address needs is also a big part of his professional life. He has learned what to look for when making donations and favors organizations that have clear reporting and communications with their donors.

When we met, Henry had just had an experience about receiving that he was still reasoning out. He and his partner had just been out to dinner with friends, a couple who have a tremendous amount of wealth. This couple is used to paying in most situations, regardless of the capability of the people they are with, and Henry had to insist to pay the bill. Henry wrestled with how to grow his friendship across the seeming barrier that their wealth created. Henry did not want to take advantage or feel beholden to them. And, as he has gotten to a place where he is comfortable in his life, he did not want his ability to provide hospitality to be discounted. Henry's story demonstrates that having friendships across economic lines is challenging, even when a surplus of money is the challenge.

---

personal level. Through this, you will understand them as resourceful in their own context. This will also help the organization's staff get to know you better so that if they need opinions, skills, or intelligence to assist them, they can ask you for those things specifically.

The challenge here is to understand our own motivations for giving in general as well as for giving to a specific cause, person, or organization. If you can take care of your own need for recognition, for control, and for feeling good about yourself elsewhere, then you can have a more generous and altruistic intent as a donor and make a greater difference to the causes you care about.

Deeper, Richer Benefits

Let's look at the benefits you might expect as a donor, which are deeper and richer than material goods, influence, or status. This may help you consider the needs you are trying to address through your giving and fulfill them more directly. Deeper benefits hearken back to the classic definition of philanthropy, "loving humankind." Those include feeling good about yourself for contributing something, or enjoying the improvements that result from your contributions. The benefits might include honoring someone you love, expressing a passion, or finding greater meaning in your life. Many people look for ways to feel good about themselves, for more meaning and satisfaction in their lives. Here is a way to gain those things. It is concrete, enduring, and relatively easy to do—take a generous approach in giving your financial resources.

There is evidence from neurological studies that being generous, just through the act of giving itself, will make you happy.[26] Psychology researchers like Elizabeth Dunn and others have found that altruistic financial behavior such as gift-giving and charitable donations promotes happiness.[27] Psychologically, one reason that giving can be so satisfying is that it makes us feel more connected to others.[28] Connection to others has been linked to happiness, health, and even life expectancy. There are many other studies that demonstrate that giving has intrinsic benefits.

Consider the warm glow effect of donor motivation. This idea originated with the economist James Andreoni.[29] In simple terms, people do not give money simply to be altruistic—to try to affect some issue they are concerned about, such as domestic abuse. They are also motivated to give to feel the glow from the act of giving—for instance, being the kind of person who is helping to curb domestic violence. They can consider themselves to be people who act selflessly and in a socially responsible way. The warm glow effect was borne out repeatedly in the interviews for this book. As Henry (p. 136) explains,

> The thing I would like to teach people about giving is to do it not just because it is the right thing, but that giving can be a self-fulfilling, loving, uplifting thing to do for yourself as well as for others.

During a time when work was consuming him and stressing him to the point where he was not sleeping and was not acting as his best self with his family, Daniel (p. 70) found real joy in helping a stranger. He said, "I looked forward to it; my son looked forward to it. We were getting so much out of it." Daniel is now a full-time volunteer and finds his new lifestyle satisfying. When people tell him that he's retired, he says, "That is not true. I am just not getting cash for it but I am paid very, very well."

Brad (p. 164) had a passion for building cooperation between nations, growing out of his experiences in the Great Depression and World War II. He has given a considerable amount of time and money to organizations that addressed the issue. His reasons included giving himself a clear purpose and a lifetime of meaningful tasks, and developing his knowledge in the subject. He said that he does not think of himself as particularly brilliant or socially adept: "Obviously I am not going to be a big politician or leader of industry." Engaging with nonprofits allowed him to feel he was doing good works with his resources.

Giving also provides a way to manifest one's beliefs and priorities in the world. Barry (p. 56) said it this way:

For me, being charitable is an opportunity to affirm, in a real way, what I believe in and to demonstrate it materially in the world. It is me being willing to actually underwrite it, putting my money where my mouth is.

Another deeper benefit of generosity is the opportunity to better match the way we behave in the world with the person we hope to be—our best selves. Amy-Lee, (p. 108) a young adult just beginning this exploration, expresses it in this way:

Giving my time and my money intentionally is a way of helping me to become the person I have always wanted to be. I want that more than anything and it pushes me to do it—to become a better person.

Being a donor can also enrich your engagement with the issue and allow you to take part in public dialogue about that issue in a way that you would not otherwise. This was Henry's experience, especially when he gave to political causes, which were among his core concerns. He said,

Being charitable gives you credibility and access. You have a "share of voice," "street cred." When you are in a discussion, you can say, "Look I have been there, I have been involved and I understand what is going on. I've paid my dues; I have made an investment of my time and money."

These examples might spark your own consideration. What have you noticed that you gain by being altruistic in your giving? What kind of recognition for your giving means the most to you? When have you experienced empowerment as a result of your giving?

Finally on this topic, Henry's description of what he expects in return for his giving seem indispensably wise. He said,

You cannot always expect reciprocity or a thank you for your giving. That can't deter you. It is like a relationship with your spouse, your kids, or your parents; every moment with them cannot be a perfect moment. That is true with being a volunteer or giving money as well.

Informed Giving

To be a skillful and generous giver, you will need to gather some information about the organizations you hope to support, and understand how that data is normally expressed. Many resources help with this.

One set of data often held up to assess a nonprofit's effectiveness is its overhead costs—also termed administrative costs, fundraising or development costs, or cost to raise a dollar. Nonprofits are aware of this and of the fact that some popular donor resource websites (listed below) use this data to rate their performance. Because of this, nonprofits present their information in the best possible light, hoping to gain, or at least not lose, donors. Some organizations use this information as a marketing message; for example, "Less than 3 percent of the value of your donation is used for overhead." This probably harms nonprofit organizations who try to unduly limit their administrative costs. After all, these costs include maintenance of the systems that make it possible to manage their programs, continuing education for its staff, communications expenses, and even some research. For the donor, this is also a poor measure of effectiveness or even efficiency, if taken on its own. In some instances, a nonprofit is being so effective that they purposefully increase their administrative expenses to expand the geographic area where they provide services, or update their computer systems to that they can better track the outcomes of their programs. If you are going to be an intelligent giver, you will need to do some deeper research. Communicating directly with the organization will help.

As a donor, you have some basic choices to consider. You may want to make a few donations with the largest amount you can, or you may want to make donations to groups of nonprofits that address your area of concern with different strategies. Your focus area may be local, regional, national, or international. You may look for smaller, less well-funded charities, so you can make a larger impact with the size of donation you are giving. Or you may want to fund larger organizations that have more financial resilience and ability to pilot new initiatives. Some organizations have been able to build larger reserves. This, again, is not a good measure of their effectiveness or potential for your donation being well-used. All nonprofits should have regular audits from an outside evaluator, the results of which are usually presented to their board and are available if you need that level of surety.

In order to make sure your efforts are well-guided, you want to be sympathetic and to understand the issues and people you are concerned about, so it is important to learn as much as you can about them. This may present you with more choices. If you are passionate about helping mothers who are victims of domestic violence, the nonprofits that address that problem will approach it with different strategies. Some might set up safe houses where escaping families can stay. Some may provide education, counseling, and a hotline to at-risk women. Others might educate young women about domestic violence as part of a broader education program; or they might work in advocacy to create more effective laws, enforcement, or funding for domestic-violence programs. They may even work with the violent partners to try to reduce violence where it starts. When you educate yourself, you will be able to decide what you believe are the best strategies, so you know where to direct your gifts.

Engagement is the key; you should try to match your heart and your resources. It is natural to volunteer for organizations where you are making a substantial financial contribution; that is where you focus your passion. Volunteering may also be the best way to learn directly about charitable organizations. That way, you will find out how they work, who they work with, and what the people they serve think about their effectiveness.

Before you dive into engagement, start by doing some research into nonprofits. You will want to find out what strategies they use to address an issue, which of these align with your values and are most effective, and who is doing them well. You can do this research at a library, on the Internet, or by interviewing people about them. Some of the better-known websites for identifying areas of concern and the organizations that address them are:

- GreatNonprofits, which gathers and posts user experiences, not expert reviews, to help you find and share information about nonprofits (www.greatnonprofits.org).
- Philanthropedia (a division of Guidestar), which lists nonprofits categorized by topic area, ranks them, and gives reviews (www.myphilanthropedia.org).
- A few U.S. cities have a Catalogue for Philanthropy, which gathers applications from local nonprofits and enlists reviewers from the local community to help evaluate them (www.catalogueforphilanthropy.org/natl).

Once you find an organization that you want to know more about, and possibly donate to, go to their website or contact them to request written materials. Consult a form called an IRS Form 990, which is an annual reporting document that provides information on the organization's mission, programs, and finances. Next, look for their Annual Report. This should give you richer detail about what they do, how they do it, and their costs.

Some donor-information websites can help with finding a nonprofit's Form 990 and with evaluating them as well. They look at data and use professionals to analyze and rate their effectiveness. These might also be a source for finding nonprofits as well.

- Charity Navigator, a well-known online evaluator, focuses on financial aspects such as overhead (www.charitynavigator.org).

- Guidestar is the oldest and perhaps largest database and online tool for evaluative data of nonprofits (www. guidestar.org).
- Givewell provides in-depth studies of nonprofit effectiveness in a limited number of issue areas (www. givewell.org).

New tools are being developed all the time. Be sure to do a general search on the web as part of your research to find any new tools or search engines to utilize.

All of these sites will help you to establish that the nonprofit organization is legitimate and established, and that it has tax-exempt status with the IRS as a 501(c)(3). If the organization has this status, then it is subject to requirements by the IRS, such as making its Form 990 available and being prohibited from supporting political candidates. Your financial contributions to these organizations are usually tax-deductible.

It is difficult to assess, based on data, the positive effect that tax deductibility has on charitable donations. However, it is generally agreed that the charitable deduction is an important and effective incentive for giving, strengthening the nonprofit sector's capacity to meet its mission ends. For many years, lawmakers have discussed potential incentives for charitable giving in the tax code. You may want to follow and contribute to this discussion.

There are many ways that you can give money to make positive changes in the world and benefit other people. Some of them are not tax-deductible—examples include giving money to a relative who is not your dependent, giving money to a stranger on the street, or directly assisting a family in need. In practicing openhearted and open-handed generosity, don't limit yourself solely by the tax advantages that charitable giving might provide.

Henry is a mature and sophisticated donor who also works for a charitable organization. During our interview, he spoke about how he gives from his intellect and from his heart:

The things that make me hesitant to give to certain non-profit organizations are if they don't have a clear mission, goals, and objectives, they do not have processes in place to help me understand their accountability. I want to know where and how the money I give is being spent, who is deciding these things, and what the results were of their efforts. It needs to be quantified and understandable.

I have different standards for different causes, some ruled by head and some the heart; I think most people want a combination of both. I have an emotional connection like I do to my church, my political causes, and my university. My giving is different with them; I am a little less rigorous about it but tend to get more involved, give more of my time. As I do things for them, I become more eager to understand what is going on. With those I try not to get too demanding and exacting. I give money to my university soccer team and I really don't know where it is going, but I have a very warm spot in my heart for that team.

Strategies for Your Philanthropic Plan

Now that you have more information about how to be skillful in your role as a nonprofit donor, let us lay out elements of strategy to consider.

You have many options to consider as you plan your giving. You can plan to be generous this year, in the coming years, and possibly as part of your legacy after you are deceased. Most people give one-time donations as their first gift, or where they do not have a strong connection. You might also make an annual or multiyear gift to a nonprofit, or a perpetual gift, which continues until you stop it. The recipient organization can usually help you set these up. You might consider a large, or major, gift depending on your priorities. And you may want to use some of the many opportunities of a planned gift.[30] These include setting up a trust that returns income to you as the donor in return for the contribution. There are many of these types of instruments; they are developed and adapted all the time. The major ones have defined structures, restrictions, and tax benefits. They are known as charitable remainders, unitrusts, annuities, and charitable lead trusts. You can also include legacy gifts in your plan, which will be given after your death. These may also involve a trust you set up, assignations in your retirement plan or in life insurance. The simplest and most common form of legacy gift is through your personal will. No matter how modest your resources or your stage of life, you should have a will to ensure that your wishes are carried out after your death. Because of the legal and tax implications of planned gifts, you will probably need to talk to a lawyer, tax accountant, or financial planner to effectively implement this part of your plan.

In addition, ensure that your practice includes the flexibility to be generous when you encounter a need, even if is not in your plan. Amy-Lee is doing this, and spoke about what led her to that tactic:

> What I have been doing is to give to First Parish [her congregation] with a sense of that relationship. Then a charity will call me and I give something to them. Then at the end of the year, when I was working on my taxes, I was sometimes surprised by the gifts that I had made. It seemed kind of random; $100 here and there. I am tired of this piecemeal way which does not allow me to prioritize my values through my giving. So I now realize I need to put down a percentage for how much money I want to give away every year, make it part of my total financial planning. As part of that, I am including a budget for gifts that are responsive to requests that come up. These will not exceed a certain amount and will accord with my larger priorities.

You have many resources from which you can draw. These include your time and talents, your financial resources in their many forms, and your ability to help form a community of concern about the issues that call to you. The latter might mean making introductions among people you know, so they can leverage each other's resources.

Financially, you might give from a number of resource "pots." One of these is your income stream. You can donate part of your monthly income in the form of a payroll deduction, which your employer may have available or which you can set up through your own bank. Alternatively, you can set up an account with regular deposits for charitable purposes or you can give directly from your available funds. If your income is variable, you will have to make additional projections to account for that. You can also make donations from investments, such as stocks and bonds or business interest. This might also include gifts from an Individual Retirement Account (IRA) or other retirement savings. You can also give or lend from your possessions, such as real estate, jewelry, or vehicles. Each of these has different advantages toward your tax filings, so you may need to seek the advice of a tax lawyer, tax accountant, or certified financial planner, or do some of your own investigation on the web.[31] Many people find they are able to give much more than they expected when they consider all their resources and use creativity in shifting them around to accommodate their giving.

As you consider your giving strategy, you may decide to help people with urgent survival needs, help them maintain their current level of sustenance, or help make systemic changes. Philosopher and author Peter Singer believes we should make moral decisions in a coolly scientific manner rather than relying on intuitions, laws, or religious guidelines.[32] Over several decades, he has contributed an increasing share of his income to organizations that address the urgent needs of people living in poverty overseas. He says he now gives about one-third of his income to such causes. "The first donation was the hardest to make," he says. "The first time I wrote a check that had at least a couple of zeroes at the end—that was the hardest thing." And yet when Singer passes a homeless person on the street, he stops himself from giving anything because the same money can produce more well-being overall when channeled through a group. What will you do in your plan—give from a scientific perspective or from your intuition, emotions, or religious beliefs? There are no clear and absolute "best practices" here; you must decide based on your own values.

When you think about the people or issues you hope to affect, and how to tailor your giving strategy accordingly, make sure you do so with applicable and current information. Different concerns or populations have different needs; these needs, in turn, are best met by a variety of generous measures. These include ongoing investments to create systemic change, providing the necessary tools to alter situations, create better sustainability, and buoy individual spirits. Another type is rapid response giving for urgent and basic subsistence needs—this is life-sustaining help for people enduring a crisis. Still another is financial support that is constant, without needing to see substantial improvement or change. This type of giving applies to causes and people who will always need to rely on the support of others, due to disability or other permanent circumstances. Whether you look to effect systemic change, ameliorate a short-term crisis, or provide enduring support, your plan should reflect your approach.

Among your other options, you may want to help combat environmental and other global problems that affect all species. You may also want to consider strategies that will support educational, political, or cultural causes. This book focuses on helping other *people* in need, as it is unwieldy to include all other important causes and issues. Consider a broad set of strategy options, including ones that affect everyone's quality of life, such as the arts, culture, and ecological preservation.

Expect to spend time keeping apprised of your issues of concern and tracking the activities of the organizations you support in various ways. Because of these time commitments, you may want to consider how many organizations you support. Once you give to an organization and they have your contact information, you will receive communications regularly. If you want to cut down on the solicitations, newsletter, and reports you receive, you can let those organizations know your preferences or direct your gifts to a limited number of nonprofits. Tom (p. 40) said that his wife writes many small checks to lots of local organizations. She reads all the materials they send and is careful, as well as broad, in her giving strategy. Tom, meanwhile, limits his giving to a short list of organizations because he feels more assured that the donations will be used well. These different patterns work well for Tom and his wife, and yet he also said, "If I had a lot more money, I wouldn't give to more charities; I would give larger gifts to the ones I fund now."

Sometimes, you will start on a giving initiative and eventually you realize you have to think differently about it or change course. Katherine Lorenz, who is the president of her family's foundation, The George & Cynthia Mitchell Foundation, had this experience. When she was younger and not engaged in the work of the foundation, she lived in a rural part of Mexico and started a nonprofit

---

Posthumous

Would it surprise you to learn
that years beyond your longest
    winter
you still get letters from your bank,
    your old
philanthropies, cold flakes drifting
through the mail-slot with your
    name?
Though it's been a long time since
    your face
interrupted the light in my door-
    frame,
and the last tremblings of your voice
have drained from my telephone
    wire,
from the lists of the likely, your name
is not missing. It circles in the
    shadow-world
of the machines, a wind-blown
    ghost. For generosity
will be exalted, and good credit
outlasts death. Caribbean cruises,
    recipes,
low-interest loans. For you who
    asked
so much of life, who lived acutely
even in duress, the brimming world
awaits your signature. Cancer and
    heart disease
are still counting on you for a cure.
B'nai Brith numbers you among the
    blessed.
They miss you. They want you back.
                    Jean Nordhaus

there to provide direct assistance to individual farmers who were part of her community. As a result of her greater exposure to their challenges, she realized that the issues her organization was trying to address were actually the result of more global problems. Since then, she has shifted her priorities to dedicate herself to issues of climate change, addressing the needs of the same population with different strategies and on a different scale.[33]

A final note about planning strategies: Being a loyal donor to an organization over time is valuable to that nonprofit and has benefits for you as well. With that history, you can learn more about the organization and its staff and volunteers, and you can become part of its evolution. You can grow your knowledge about the issue and how the nonprofit addresses it. And their staff can get to know you better as well, so the fit between you can improve over time. At first you will not make long-term commitments to organizations, which is appropriate. As you become more engaged, you may plan to maintain those relationships over time.

Collective Giving

You can join with others as you consider your philanthropic plan. A good way to do this, no matter your level of resources, is to set up or join a giving circle, which was described in chapter 7. Another option for collective giving is a community foundation.[34] There is a community foundation (sometimes called a "charitable foundation") in almost every area of the United States. Community foundations create and manage funds and make grants based on their donors' desires. If you or your family sets up your own fund through a community foundation, you can choose the level of control your family has over the purposes and allocations of the fund, which is usually tied to the amount of contribution to the fund. Funds with a larger contribution level and a greater level of control are called Donor Advised Funds. In some instances, like the services of a professional philanthropic advisor, these are suitable for people with larger amounts to give away. A commercial bank or stock brokerage can also set up a donor advised fund for you. As important difference between a bank or stock brokerage and a community foundation is that the community foundation is usually well informed about needs and is often familiar with the nonprofits and their effectiveness in their geographic area. They also provide expertise to donors, connect givers to the right programs, and help inform donors on emerging issues. Commercial banks or brokerages do not usually offer this assistance.

Your giving plan—and, in fact, all of your financial giving—might have an effect on your family (however broadly you define "family"). This includes giving to family members and group giving with family members. As mentioned above, Tom and his wife have different strategies for giving. This works for them, yet in many families diverse approaches might cause tensions. Likewise, the scale, form, or organizational choice for giving may take negotiating among family members (see the discussion of the Mondavi family in chapter 5).

The same holds true for one's estate—the property and assets left after one dies. Some parents may set up charitable funds that their children, because they have different priorities, may not want to carry forward. And there may be concerns about the quantity left to a nonprofit instead of to family inheritance. This might call for someone who can address these family dynamics or, in extreme cases, for mediation. To avoid some of these concerns, it is best to be open and frank with your family members as you plan, before anything is put into action. Although some people find it uncomfortable to talk about money with their family members, it is worthwhile to embark on this task.

In the last chapter I discussed financial giving that is not tax-deductible. That might include giving to family members who are in need, yet are not your financial dependents. Brad learned this attitude of financial generosity from an uncle who, although he was considered a "black sheep," still benefited future generations of his family:

An uncle of mine left money in his will to benefit each of his nieces' and nephews' education. I saw him only twice in my life. My mother didn't like him; he had a fight with my grandfather. Yet, he felt he had an obligation. I was the beneficiary and I did nothing to earn it. The money that I have is not really due to my own earning of it; that has enabled me to be generous.

Your family might also consider strategies where you give collectively. In essence, you could form a giving circle with just family members. For this, you can set up a fund with a community foundation, as mentioned above. If you have substantial collective resources, you can set up a private family foundation, although this requires management and other administration. You might set up a family fund with a bank or with a stockbroker, through which the family can then make decisions about allocating for charitable purposes. For giving within the family, you can gather family contributions and set up a savings fund to make low—or no-interest loans to family members. You also might set up structured college-savings funds. They normally name a specific beneficiary (the person who will go to college), yet anyone can contribute to the fund, including non-family members.

Your instruction, modeling, and cooperation will help shape the next generations of your family (however you define that group). If you do not share and discuss your financial generosity, you deprive your loved ones of learning opportunities. For more detail on ways to provide learning in a community setting, see chapter 7.

When you become a more informed, engaged, conscientious, and strategic giver, you make donations that create the change you are seeking—in yourself, in the causes you care about, and in the world. This will create benefits for you as a donor, and your example may help lead others to join in a community of concern and collective giving. That way, the nonprofits you care about become more sustainable and deliver better results.

PRACTICES

Research Nonprofits

When you reach out in an effort to inform yourself about organizations, the organizations themselves do not have to spend as much effort and resources trying to engage you. Spend some time learning more deeply about a nonprofit. You may already be a donor and a volunteer for this organization, or it may be new to you. If it is new to you, choose one that addresses something you care about. Look at their materials on the web, request printed materials about their mission, and call up their office and talk to someone about what they do. Here are some questions you may want to answer:

- What is their underlying approach to the problem, and how did they choose that approach? For instance, if the issue is hunger, they may directly supply food, work to improve sustainable food sources for specific populations, or try to develop the economy in that region so less people go hungry.
- Where and how do they directly connect with the beneficiaries of their mission (people, animals, environments, arts, or cultural change)?
- How do they gain financial resources to fuel their mission, and how well is that working?
- What do they say they need most to make a difference in their mission activities?
- How do they know that they are successful? What is their process for identifying these indicators?

Journaling

With the information you gathered in chapter 7, if you have a core community or community of practice, consider your own community:

- How is it different from another nonprofit to which you may have contributed?
- How might you give differently to your core community than to other charities and causes?

These are not easy questions, but know that you can experiment and shift until you arrive at what seems to align with the rest of your life.

If you do not have a core community, consider how you give to causes that might improve your own life in a secondary way. For instance, if you give to a museum or symphony, you benefit from enjoying the artwork produced. Or if you give to a medical nonprofit that addresses a condition you have, you may indirectly benefit from their work.

CHAPTER 9

Solidarity, Justice Giving, and Interdependence

In the 1940s, in reaction to some of the rural development practices brought to Sri Lanka by Westerners, D.A. Abeysekera started a movement based on native beliefs called *Shramadana*. The word literally means sharing of one's time, thought, and energy for the welfare of all. Although focused on improving nutrition and agriculture in undeveloped areas, the members of the movement also saw it as a way to build up an ideal social order, which they called *sarvodaya*.[35] In this new order, they hoped to see an awakening of the individual (*purna paurushodaya*), an awakening of the village (*gramodaya*), an awakening of the nation (*deshodaya*), and an awakening of the world community (*vishvodaya*). For these Sri Lankans, *sarvodaya* (new social order) intent and *shramadana* (generous) action are inseparable and dependent upon each other. In *Shramadana*, each person plays a role in conceptualizing a type of social change, as well as designing its implementation, working directly to achieve it, and benefitting from the change once it comes about.

This concept of *Shramadana* captures the essence of the purpose of this book: to inform and awaken you as a philanthropist, to help you understand how you can build intelligence individually and as part of a community, to help create a better world through your skills as a generous giver, and to point to the deeper benefits you might expect. If the origin of your generosity—your interiority—is both clear in purpose and sensitive to the humanity and conditions of the people you hope to benefit, then the rest of the process toward skillful giving will be more gracious and effective. So I recommend working to build awareness of your own values, objectives, and desires before setting strategies and creating a philanthropic plan. We must also raise our consciousness and intelligence about conditions in our world, so we better understand the issues that concern us most and can shift our perspectives and change. This will build solidarity with those we hope to benefit and will allow us to engage more skillfully, be better givers, and make the greatest difference in the world.

This chapter presents information about economic disparity in America. This understanding can help inform us about our shared circumstances. We can act as supporters and allies in solidarity across economic lines—described as *justice giving* by the Jesuit author John C. Haughey[36]—so these topics are also covered. Included here is some general guidance about how to use our money in this way.

At the end of this chapter you will find a form to fill out which will help you develop a philanthropic plan. Before you start on that, we will consider the giving-receiving dynamic, which is presented near the end of this chapter. Understanding the dynamic qualities of your giving may make you more bold and ambitious with your plan, knowing that during those engagements you will also be a recipient, and have the opportunity to build your social network in the process.

Economic Disparity

In the United States, the income gap between the middle class and people living in poverty has not changed much in recent years.[37] Meanwhile, the gap between the rich and everyone else has grown steadily and enormously since the 1970s. Even among people considered rich, there is such great disparity that a report by the economists Emmanuel Saez and Thomas Piketty divided the rich group into three categories.[38] Income gaps affect not just the amount people have to spend, but also education, health and nutrition, employment, and many other factors. Countries with greater gaps, like ours, tend to have less economic mobility.

Economic mobility—the ability to shift one's economic status as measured by income—has decreased for people in poverty. Studies show that 42 percent of American men raised in the bottom fifth of incomes remain in that income bracket as adults. That is less mobility than comparably developed countries.[39] This, in effect, traps low-income people. It can be attributed to inequities in our education and health systems, among others, so poor children start far behind their more affluent peers. The safety net programs in the United States, such as food assistance, affordable housing, and financial assistance, are less robust than in other rich countries, leaving poorer children more vulnerable. American employers pay significantly more to people with college degrees, and children generally gain the same level of education as their parents, so poorer young people lose opportunities for higher wages. Recent studies show that a third of Americans raised in the middle class (between the 30th and 70th percentiles of the income distribution) fall out of the middle class as adults. Race, marital status, education, and gender all influence the ability to retain middle-class status.[40]

Many people who are on the margins of poverty are afraid. Yet in our hard and uncertain economic times, many middle-class people who are not at financial risk are also nervous about their situations. This generalized fear has prevented many from doing things they might otherwise have done, including giving

> The word *tzedakah* is derived from the Hebrew root *tzade-dalet-qof*, meaning "righteousness," "justice," or "fairness." In Judaism giving to the poor is not viewed as a generous, magnanimous act; it is simply an act of justice and righteousness.
>
> Zagloul Kadah and
> Danny Kadah

charitably. This apprehension may come from being in the group that does have more mobility, both downward and upward. Children born into the middle class experience the greatest economic mobility—as adults they move up, down, and stay put roughly in even thirds.[41]

Meanwhile, affluent families tend to transmit their advantages. More than half of Americans raised in the top fifth of income levels stay in or near that level, according to research by the Pew Charitable Trusts.[42] This in part can be attributed to their access to better educational systems. They spend more money on education, they tend to have a greater understanding of those systems, and their children are often better prepared to learn. The rich tend to stay rich from generation to generation, and the poor tend to stay poor.

This does not negate the hard work and skill of those who improve their financial status, and the organizations trying to affect upward mobility. Nor does it discount the boldness of those who choose to intentionally live more simply. Nevertheless, when people try to shift out of a socioeconomic level, they face special struggles.

Our culture seems conflicted about these issues. We are both curious and opinionated about socioeconomic status. We make people celebrities just because they are rich. As depicted in popular media, it appears that people who are wealthy have lives filled with ease and free time; they are clothed and surrounded by beauty, catered to at every turn. We seem to be nearly universally enthralled in a fantasy of great wealth. Yet we Americans also like to think of ourselves as anti-elitist. This is such a part of our social norms that financial status, although a part of many interactions, is usually subtle and unspoken. It is generally considered impolite to ask people about financial transactions, considered gossip to talk about another's financial resources, and considered rude to flaunt one's money. The emergence of the Occupy Movement demonstrates how angry so many people are at the wealthy "1 percent" and at economic disparity in the United States. According to studies by the Pew Research Center, about two-thirds of the public believe there are "very strong" or "strong" conflicts between the rich and poor, a greater amount than seen in conflicts regarding immigration, race, and age.[43]

People with surplus resources may try to set themselves apart by living in gated communities, isolating themselves through their work environments, and joining social clubs with people like themselves. This may emanate from a desire to protect themselves from thieves and scammers. Sometimes, people find that their socioeconomic level affects their values, beliefs, and viewpoints, and they gravitate toward others who share similar perspectives. For instance, people with similar financial resources may share political views, ideas about education, or social values. But homogeneous settings can also isolate their members and fail to provide warm community. Any exclusive community, regardless of financial bracket, makes it difficult to know or be in relationship with people from diverse backgrounds.

Paul Piff, a social psychologist at the University of California at Berkeley, has conducted studies showing that as wealth increases, people become more insulated, less likely to get involved with people, and less attuned to the suffering of others.[44] Social psychologist Paul Schervish explains that what is fundamentally different about most of the world's wealthy is the closed and insular social world they inhabit.[45] Because they tend to separate themselves into suburban and gated communities, members of high-income households are less likely to witness someone in need. In neighborhoods where more than 40 percent of households reported earning $200,000 or more, each household donated just 2.8 percent of disposable income on average, compared with the 4.2 percent donated by all households that itemized on their tax returns and earned more than $200,000.[46]

However, class differences dissolved in research Paul Piff conducted in which both wealthy and lower-income participants were required to watch a short video about childhood poverty.[47] As Paul Schervish interprets these results: "Simply seeing someone in need at the grocery store—or looking down the street at a neighbor's modest home—can serve as basic psychological reminders of the needs of other people. Absent that, wealth will have these egregious effects, insulating you more and more."

This is, in fact, the story of how Prince Siddhartha Gautama became the Buddha. He spent most of his early life living in a palace, well-protected in opulent surroundings and shielded from a view of suffering of all kinds. When he was a young husband and father, he left his palace to meet his subjects. On this trip, which led to more trips beyond the palace gates, he encountered the various sufferings of humans and other living creatures. This led him to abandon the palace and live as an ascetic for many years, followed by a period of intense meditation resulting in his enlightenment. He then became a teacher upon whose ideas and practices Buddhism was founded. Quite simply, once he saw the suffering outside his gated community, he was called to reflection and action.

This book's interviewees revealed that exposure to the suffering of others changed the course of their lives as well. Brad (p. 164) lived most of his life in privilege and comfort. He was a child during the Great Depression and, while his father lost his job and was unemployed for a while, their family did not endure real hardship. However, Brad saw people suffering. "There were a lot of unfortunate people around," he said. This may have given him compassion for people who are less fortunate, and supported his lifelong giving to end war and promote cooperation between nations. Tom (p. 40) grew up going to elite schools and his father was a corporate leader. Right out of college, he served in the Peace Corps and was exposed to people in need in South America. Rather than return and go to law school or into the diplomatic corps, which had been his plan, he stayed in international development and has had a career in the nonprofit sector ever since.

People who are financially comfortable sometimes intentionally conceal the signs of their affluence. In fact, an enormous number of people define themselves as "middle class." According to survey statistics from the National Opinion Research Center at the University of Chicago, a significant number of Americans define themselves as "working class" or "middle class."[48] Their large survey showed that 50 percent of families who earn between $20,000 and $40,000 annually, 38 percent of families who earn between $40,000 and $60,000 annually, and 16.8 percent of those families who earn more than $110,000 annually characterize themselves this way.

In light of these statistics, consider how economically homogenous your community is. Also consider other diversity factors, including race and sexual preference. How much time and care do you spend with people in your own social class? When we masquerade as "middle-class" when we're not, we conceal the true issues of disparity, affecting charitable giving behavior, preventing ourselves from being authentic with each other, and inhibiting the building of true solidarity.

Solidarity

Solidarity—unity or agreement in feeling or action, with mutual support—is a central concept of social justice work. In economic terms, it is "a basic principle of social economy, meaning interdependence, redistribution, and joint responsibility."[49]

Our role in creating solidarity could include finding ways to unite with others in mutual support to create a more just world. We stand "shoulder to shoulder" with those we hope to benefit with our charitable giving. It is not so much fixing, supporting, or even serving; it is being in kinship. It is "loving human-kind" (philanthropy); this avoids judgments and builds social connections.

As resource-rich people, we hold the power to bridge the cultural and economic divisions in our society. What can help us to do that? What can allow us to be open-hearted in economically diverse situations—where we may fear being scorned, robbed, taken advantage of, or just be anxious about clashes in culture? Instead of sheltering behind systems and go-betweens and remaining behind the "walls" of privilege, we can find other ways to navigate.

One approach is to be aware of, and challenge, the cultural privilege our level of resources provides us. Another is to understand that economic diversity carries with it cultural differences, and approach interactions with people from other classes as multicultural experiences. A third is to create personal relationships with people from diverse economic backgrounds, and certainly those whom we hope to benefit. Our approach should be to help people achieve a level of financial independence and security, where they are free from the need to seek support. Educator and philosopher Paolo Freire expressed it this way:

> True generosity consists precisely in fighting to destroy the causes which nourish false charity. False charity constrains the fearful and subdued, the "rejects of life" to extend their trembling hands. True generosity lies in striving so that these hands—whether of individuals or entire peoples— need be extended less and less in supplication, so that more and more they become human hands which work and, working, transform the world.[50]

Another crucial element to building solidarity is to believe firmly that the people we benefit are resourceful and, with mutually given support, can change their circumstances. This is to have a humanist approach that emphasizes the value and agency of human beings, individually and collectively. A humanist approach might be chosen over a humanitarian one, which employs an ethic of kindness, benevolence, and sympathy extended universally and impartially to all.

This speaks to the need to act and think with humility. Some of our great twentieth-century leaders such as Mother Teresa, Mahatma Gandhi, and Martin Luther King Jr. created enormous change in the world by doing what they thought was right and best for all people—although they focused on the disenfranchised and powerless. Even though they became important international figures—sometimes coming up from among the same groups they championed—they each did this in a humble and personal way that retained the solidarity with the people for whom they struggled.

Another factor that helps to create solidarity with others is recognizing the commonalities we share. When we acknowledge that each socioeconomic level brings with it its own challenges, and that these levels are usually not chosen and tend to reinforce themselves, we are more able to connect with people. Everyone has basic human needs for survival, meaning, and belonging. Everyone also has individual strengths and resources, regardless of their financial or other circumstances. Anthony (p. 90) expresses this well:

> I don't think you can look around and not see that things are really unequal, unfair, and unethical. Although I grew up with the strong message that people have to pull themselves up by the bootstraps, at the same time I believe in fairness. We don't necessarily create our own situation, sometimes problems just happen, so you have to just help others. I know that some people have a lot, but sometimes even *they* do not have the things that they need.

In order to build solidarity, it is vital not to rely on generalizations, ideas from childhood, or false beliefs. Some of the biases we carry are based on stereotypes that are pervasive, yet are not applicable when people are understood as individuals. This is an act of seeing people in a new way. Elise (p. 56) remembers a lesson her father taught her:

> My father used to say to us as kids, sitting around a restaurant table, "Don't forget that waitress is not just supporting herself, she's got a lot of other people she is supporting and feeding. That is not just one person standing there, it is a whole family or group of people she needs to help support."

text continues on page 166

BRAD

We live in an irrevocable, interconnected, Internet world, with problems which no country can solve alone.

—Brad

Brad was unlike anyone else I interviewed. He was born into a wealthy family, inheriting considerable wealth; and he was older than anyone else: in his mid-nineties. We met at a restaurant near his home in an affluent suburb, and later sat talking in his comfortable house. This reflected the fact that he was still active and engaged in many activities, like someone decades younger.

Although he was a child during the Depression, saw much deprivation, and experienced his father being out of work for a time, he seems to lack the conservatism and financial security concerns that are common among people who lived during the 1930s. However, living through a world war and our subsequent overseas conflicts, he realized that the build-up of the defense industry was reallocating funds that otherwise could fight hunger, improve health, and provide housing and parks. He also saw that war could be reduced by creating more cooperation between nations, utilizing institutions such as the United Nations. In fact, Brad felt that collaborating on functions of governance across the globe would solve most of our major problems as a human race.

After a certain point in his life Brad did not have to work for a living, and he dedicated himself to this cause. He volunteered in organizations, served on many boards, and became an active donor with a broad portfolio of giving relationships. This gave him a sense of purpose, a role to play, and lent meaning to the happenstance of his birth into a wealthy family.

Perhaps because he had lived so long, Brad was acutely aware of how the world had become connected in a way that was impossible before. He said that we could not act as if something that was happening elsewhere in the world would not affect us here in America. "We have cured tuberculosis in America, yet if someone has TB anywhere in the world they can get on a plane and be here in a number of hours. We no longer have the luxury of being insular."

For more than seventy years, this issue has dominated his professional life, his charitable giving, and his volunteering. He has set up more than ten charitable trusts that benefited nonprofit organizations working to breach the divisions between nations. He said, "I think they are the best investment you can make."

One of Brad's great apprehensions was about his children and grandchildren and their learning to be charitable. Although their inheritances have been planned and he has provided well for them, his effort to engage them had not yielded the results that Brad would have hoped. Not only were their concerns different from Brad's, but they resisted his attempts to involve them in his charitable giving, which saddened him.

My father is also very generous in hotels when leaving a tip for the maids. I would leave $3 and my father would say, "No, leave $10 or $20 because they are the ones who are getting underpaid in the hotel."

Multicultural Approach

We cannot join in sympathy, action, or mutual support with people we do not know. For this reason, it is essential for solidarity that we find ways to enter into relationships with some of the people we hope to benefit. It is common to feel awkward when you are in a situation or setting where you do not "fit" financially, whether the rest of the group is of a higher or lower socioeconomic status. Sometimes it seems we speak different languages and have different values; our ways of making meaning in the world and interpreting events may make those differences seem impossible to bridge. This becomes easier when you think of your exchange in cultural terms and take a multicultural approach.

When we encounter someone from a culture that is not ours, we tend to hold fewer assumptions, to be more curious, and to be less inclined to take offense based on what we might otherwise perceive as social friction. We do not discount our own reactions, but usually we know that due to cultural differences, we may not be reading others' intent accurately. Should we experience fear or discomfort in an interaction with someone from another culture, we might deal with it more easily when we assume that we will continue to inhabit our separate cultural communities and can progress at our own pace toward greater understanding.

Liz, (p. 174) who lives in areas of violent conflict overseas, is sometimes uncomfortable when dealing with work colleagues and friends due to cultural differences. Clearly, as characterized by the *Shramadana* movement at the beginning of this chapter, she is an "awakening individual." She described how her experiences have changed her:

Sometimes I feel like I am becoming less American in that sense because I am living in cultures where the give and take is much stronger. The obligations are also much stronger.

When I meet someone who is clearly from my own environs, yet from a different socioeconomic, ethnic, racial, or religious group, I find that understanding our interaction as a multicultural encounter removes some of the barriers to authentic connection. That does not mean that I am freed from my biases. As a white man, I am aware that sometimes my responses in the interaction may reflect my reacting to a potential shift of traditional roles—my privilege may be challenged, which may make me uncomfortable. My responsibility is to feel the discomfort, understand it as resulting from my cultural privilege, and be willing to be changed as Liz was. At the same time, I must be mindful of my own care, knowing that I cannot stand in solidarity if I am stuck in reactivity or unproductive guilt as a result of my inherited cultural status.

Barbara (p. 6) told a story that, like many of her stories, was remarkable because she seemed to lack any judgment about the circumstances that prompted her to offer help. She truly takes people as they are without imposing her own cultural context upon them. At the time, she was teaching and had a sixteen-year-old, low-income student whose parents got divorced. The student's father remarried a woman who had children of her own and did not want an additional child in the house, so the boy's grandmother agreed to take him. One summer his grandmother needed surgery, so she called Barbara because she did not want to leave the boy alone in the house. He stayed with Barbara for the whole summer; her family helped him get a job and took him into their family. Of this, she remarked, "It did not seem strange; it seemed like the right thing to do."

Building Relationships

Elise, who grew up in an affluent household, remembers an uncle who had an open heart and built warm and authentic relationships across economic lines in his community. He used his wealth to address directly the needs of people he knew in their own neighborhood. At the same time, he gave her experiences that put her own family circumstances in context and taught Elise valuable and enduring lessons. Elise said,

> He lived in Kansas City in a community that was all African American. Although he was a wealthy white guy, African Americans were his neighbors and friends. I remember going with him to the grocery store around the holidays. He would fill up his big Cadillac and go to these very dilapidated houses in the poorer part of the neighborhood. He would knock on doors and deliver a turkey and a brown bag full of canned goods. I was mostly struck because of the community I was seeing; I did not grow up in an area like that. I was struck by the graciousness and pride with which people accepted that food and the way they embraced my uncle. He was a hero to them; and he just loved these people, it was so clear that he loved the people of his community. To me it was not scary because of that; I was more awestruck.

Human interactions like these are powerfully essential to building solidarity and relationships across economic and other cultural divides. The popular saying holds true: "We do not fear people whose stories we know." As you develop relationships with people and attempt to build solidarity with them, try to be a careful and sympathetic listener to their stories, and to tell yours.

Think of generosity as a bridge, so you can build solidarity by sharing your resources with other people and by receiving generously as well. In fact, that relationship can blur the line between giver and receiver.

My friend Steve met Julia through his business, and even after she was no longer using his services, she would come to his workplace to see him. Steve and Julia are from different ethnic backgrounds, age groups, and economic levels. Some of Steve's family members had health problems, and Julia never failed to ask about them by name and circumstance. When Steve's mother died, Julia was the only African American to attend her funeral. When the congregation was invited to share any thoughts or memories about Steve's mother, there was a long and uncomfortable silence. Finally, Julia walked down the aisle to speak. She spoke movingly about Steve's mother, whom she had never met, and encouraged the group not to be sad because his mother was free and with God. Clearly, she was supporting Steve and helping with his mourning in those moments. Steve found it wonderful that, as odd as it seemed to him, "this Caucasian, male, upper-middle-class, gay man found a soul mate in Julia."

Then, Steve did not see Julia for a while. When he reached her by phone, he discovered that her health and finances had worsened. Because he did not want to offend her sense of independence, Steve had a check sent anonymously to her every month. Yet because elders are so often sent scams in the mail, he felt he needed to let her know the money was coming from someone who cared. He sent Julia an anonymous postcard that said—taking Julia's beliefs (not Steve's) into account—she was receiving the money because God loved her and recognized her loving spirit. Steve said, "I feel connected to the love that others have shown me by sharing what I have with Julia. The gift is unconditional, given freely. Giving Julia this gift allows me to be Love."

Part of what I find powerful about this story is that it illustrates that although different cultures have distinct norms about giving and receiving, there are benefits to cross-cultural experiences. When we enter into a relationship and gain mutual benefit, it will be most successful if both cultures of the people involved are understood, respected, and honored.

In addition to building relationships and solidarity with members of communities that are different from ours, it is just as important to find allies and mentors from our own communities to support us in this effort. The communities of practice described in chapter 7 can help us with this.

Justice Giving

Let us now look more directly at how giving can be informed by solidarity—through justice giving. There are three concepts of giving that may be useful when considering giving in a justice context. The first two come from a Judeo-Christian context: tithing and almsgiving. The third is justice giving; it is more of a secular concept, but for some, it may build upon their religious beliefs.[51] Tithing, as described in chapter 7, helped to institutionalize Judaism, taking it from a tribal cult to an established religion. The practice is employed by a number of religions today. Almsgiving, in the Christian tradition, means giving in a spontaneous, compassionate way in imitation of God's compassion for the needy (the term has different meanings in other religions). Both tithing and almsgiving have a number of potential drawbacks. They have the potential to promote a sense of righteousness in the giver. Also, they quantify one's giving. They both rely on the good will of the giver, not on what might be just for the recipient.

There are a number of different types of justice; several of which pertain to justice giving.[52] There is legal justice, which refers to the rights and responsibilities of citizens to obey the laws put forward by their government. Commutative justice refers to what is owed between individuals, as in contracts or business transactions. Distributive justice refers to the fair allocation of resources. Finally, contributive justice is the obligation of members to contribute to their group. More generally, contributive justice has to do with each person contributing to the common good of all humankind, including toward the sustainability of the planet.

Justice giving, for our purposes, combines three concepts: distributive justice, contributive justice, and a non-legal type of justice that goes back to the philosopher Aristotle. As Michael Sandel, a professor at Harvard describes it, Aristotle's idea of justice is that "justice consists in giving people what they deserve, and that a just society is one that enables human beings to realize their highest nature and to live the good life."[53] What does each person's deserve? We can argue which elements and in what quantity might be on that list. Yet certainly we would agree that no one should be subject to injustice.

Justice giving promotes a just allocation of resources. It considers what each person can contribute to the common good and takes into account what each person is due at a minimum because of their humanity. This can be more challenging than almsgiving or tithing, and it requires much more discernment.

In his "I Have a Dream" speech, Martin Luther King Jr. calls for racial justice using the metaphor of a bank check, which fits the idea of justice giving.[54] The metaphorical check in his speech promised life, liberty, and happiness to all—regardless of color. He said that black people had been given a bad check, marked "insufficient funds." But King refused to accept that the "bank of justice is bankrupt," that "great vaults of opportunity of this nation" had insufficient funds. He said that it was time to cash that check, giving

> A true vision of peace sees a continuous mutuality between giving and receiving. Let's never give anything without asking ourselves what we are receiving from those to whom we give, and let's never receive anything without asking what we have to give to those from whom we receive.
>
> Henri J.M. Nouwen

him and all people the "riches of freedom and the security of justice." One would not expect Dr. King, with his beautiful, high rhetoric, to use such a seemingly base metaphor. But it is a good one because we do actually grant freedom and justice to one another with checks and generosity. If they are deployed skillfully and with the right intent, they can help us do just that.

If you are privileged, you may find that you ask yourself, "How should I live now?" Amy-Lee (p. 108) asks herself, "What kind of daily life do I want; what are the priorities? I could always live in a smaller home, or in a less expensive neighborhood. What is reasonable for me to have for a lifestyle versus what I am giving?" These questions bring weight to your discernment, and they relate to how you define a level of comfort and financial security for yourself. They also help to direct you away from comparison and judgment of how others have adapted or made their decisions and help you prepare to build solidarity.

To be a skilled financial giver—a philanthropist in a justice context—it is worth considering your position as a donor (see chapter 8). As a donor, you are on the giving side of the charitable transaction. You are separated by your resources, by your power, and possibly by cultural and socioeconomic barriers. Generally speaking, the recipients are "the needy," and you are the provider. Cultivating yourself as an "awakening individual" will help address this discrepancy. The clearer we are with our egos and our own needs when we are giving, the more freedom we give to the people who receive our gifts. We must be careful to not impose our personal values and morals with our giving. We should not give for the purpose of assuaging our own guilt, making ourselves feel "better-than," or confirming our relative wealth. We should not give to establish or maintain our own status. Part of our giving should be done with the intent to surrender our privilege for the sake of a more just society for us all.

When you are generous to another person, you connect with them in a direct way. Yet as donors, especially when we give to international causes, we can feel far removed. The distance between you as a donor and the beneficiaries may make connection seem impossible. You are writing a check and sending it to a nonprofit, which then funds a project that benefits someone. This is a pretty long chain of connection, so it is not likely to be strong. Neither you nor the person you benefit may feel the relationship through this complex conduit. And you may not be able to maintain this connection unless you find a way to more directly relate to the people served. Still, there are ways to give in a way that can build solidarity irrespective of distance.

One way to build solidarity is to take a service trip to a developing nation. These are normally arranged through community groups and can result in long-term, affectionate relationships, as well as a way to provide material support. This can also be found in programs where donors are connected to overseas families in need, through photos and correspondence. In programs like this, the relationship can develop as normal details of the participant's lives are conveyed.

An example of this is the Leaders Educated as Philanthropists (LEAP) program.[55] This recruits students in the United States from two communities—one affluent and one non-affluent. These two groups then connect and recruit a group of kids in an overseas location, usually in the developing world, to devise and implement a social change project together. Whatever funding is needed usually comes from the students in the affluent community, although LEAP teams collaborate with professionals to generate micro-enterprise, small loans, and local businesses. This helps builds relationships and common cause among the three disparate groups, while it teaches all of them leadership and cross-cultural collaboration, and avoids the normal humanitarian aid models.

Chapter 7 described how some religions emphasize the benefits of being an anonymous giver, using Maimonides's "Ladder of Charity." Let's address anonymity as a donor again, this time from a solidarity and justice perspective.

This personal story comes from a blogger named Pilar Gonzales.[56] During a difficult period in her family's financial life, her grandparents accepted bags of groceries that were distributed through their church. In her Latino family's culture, when a giver did not reveal his or her identity it created suspicion about the giver's motives; hiding was not seen as noble. During this difficult time in their lives, the anonymous gift added to their shame. Being able to meet or know the identity of the giver would have allowed them to say thank you; this would have equalized the relationship, making it fairer and more balanced. Gonzales learned that "expressing gratitude could restore power to the recipient."

text continues on page 176

LIZ

If we are able to overcome our darker nature to help other people; then everyone can, and we can all have peace.

—Liz

Liz appears to be a typical, intelligent, young urban adult—but she is not. She works overseas doing democracy building. The country where she works is in political turmoil; she is endangered by intermittent random violence. This is what she has done for her whole career in hotspots around the globe. She talked about how she had moved from always being angry at the heedless political forces that led to violence to a perspective where she wanted to work in solidarity to make things better, starting with herself as a peaceful and helpful person. I was lucky to catch her in this country while she was staying with her parents and doing some U.S.-based volunteer work. We sat and talked at a sidewalk table, in a local coffee shop.

Because her family constantly moved around to different countries as she was growing up, they were more concerned with finding their way rather than making deep connections in those communities. For that reason, they seldom discussed charitable giving and volunteering; these were secondary considerations. However, Liz's parents did convey how important it is to stop what you are doing and provide help when it is needed; they were very generous in this regard.

When Liz was in college, a friend of hers was kidnapped for money and then murdered by someone who had just been released from jail. Her friends and, indeed, the whole school were stunned and wracked with grief, then anger. During this time, Liz had a lot of experiences of caring for others and learned that care can sometimes be exhausting in an unproductive way. Related to that murder, Liz and her friends started to learn about corruption in the prisons and started working for reform. For Liz, this was another turning point where she realized that violence does not have to be meaningless if it prompts change.

Liz told a number of stories about cultural differences in hospitality, and what is acceptable in giving and receiving in the places where she works. She described one country where the people are generous in the extreme by American standards. The local people are sophisticated and refined, which makes it difficult to tell if their motives are altruistic or self-interested. Liz said that she had ended up in situations where people had been generous to her, only to find out later that they considered it a debt in order to gain some kind of advantage. Although Liz found this a painful realization, she understood it as a cultural difference and has since learned how to navigate and still admire the generosity of the people with whom she works.

The donor might see anonymity as a virtuous, selfless way to give, but the recipient might think that the donor is using their anonymity to protect them from speculation, envy, or curiosity about their good fortune. The recipient, meanwhile, must appear in public to accept the assistance. Gonzales had to explain to her grandparents that the benefactor would not be available. They had no option but to turn their thanks to the nun who had dropped off the package. Gonzales now hopes that more people will come out of the "philanthropic closet" and become known as donors.

An element in building solidarity through giving, which has been mentioned repeatedly is to ensure that the beneficiaries are engaged and have been asked what they want and need—that what is provided will work in their context and for the purpose intended. This not only ensures that the donation is well used, but recognizes the inherent dignity in the beneficiaries. Liz frequently was close to local residents from cultures unlike her own, where she was providing support, so she probably saw the effect more directly. She spoke frankly about the challenges: "I have made some big mistakes when I thought I was helping. The older I get, the more I understand that the most important thing is to ask what is needed and not just assume that you know."

Spending in Justice-Oriented Ways

Aside from charitable contributions, there are many ways to spend and invest money in justice-oriented ways, or to help improve the environment. Once you have a good philanthropic plan and are implementing it, your next project may be to start aligning your purchases and investments with your values, beliefs, and loves. This book will not provide an exhaustive list of opportunities to do this; new tools emerge so frequently that it would quickly become outdated. Yet here is an initial list to give you an idea of some options.

There are many ways to adjust your spending behavior to directly benefit or create less harm to the environment. These might include something as simple as using more energy-efficient light bulbs or buying fair-trade goods. These can also be large changes in expenses, such as building an energy-neutral or energy-generating house. They can be changes in how you live, to conserve money as well as the environment, such as selling your car and using more public transportation.

Businesses can be part of creating a just and sustainable world. Some are already doing so. Your pressure as a client or consumer will make a big difference in corporations that are not just and sustainable. You can act as a responsible purchaser by becoming more aware of the impact your purchases have on the environment, politics, workers, and society at large. You can also take an active part in boycotting certain products or companies. You might find it time-consuming to do the extra work to source out and access ethical businesses. There are, however, some guides to assist.

Since the late 1990s, some corporations have been using full-cost accounting. This involves looking at what is termed the triple bottom line of people, planet, and profit (social, ecological, and economic performance data) for measuring organizational and societal success. Although this type of accounting has its critics, it does provide some guidance in broader corporate responsibility. Some other resources:

- The organization B Corporation rates organizations by their standards of transparency, accountability, and performance regarding impact and sustainability, using a triple-bottom-line framework. They publish a list on their web site of certified B Corps (www.bcorporation. net).
- The film company p.h. balanced films (www.phbalancedfilms.org) investigates international production and supply chains in certain business sectors to find out how consumers are impacting the world, then makes films about them to educate the public.

- Websites and smartphone apps such as Better World Shopper (www.betterworldshopper.com), allow users to search by product category and see ratings for social and environmental responsibility.

In some instances, our governance and regulatory systems have not kept pace with developments in responsible business. An example of this is certification for "organic" foods. Although demand for organic food has been exploding for decades and supply chains are international, requirements differ from country to country. The USDA has three levels of certification, which are fairly obscure for the average consumer; alternative certification systems also exist in the United States.

If you have investments, you can help make a difference in the world with those as well. This is again an area of innovation, most notably in creating investment funds that blend investing with charitable giving. Below are some starter options; you may also decide to look at an organization called Talgra (www.talgra.com), which publishes a directory of impact investing on the web. The first and most broad-based strategy to consider is shareholder advocacy, whereby you contact the companies in which you invest and ask them to account for themselves in your areas of concern. If their response is not satisfactory, you can work as an investor to create change.

In socially responsible investing (SRI), people steer their investing toward corporations whose practices promote environmental stewardship, consumer protection, human rights, and diversity. Some investment options also avoid businesses involved in industries not considered humane or sustainable, such as alcohol, tobacco, or weapons. Many companies are solely focused on SRI; many investment banks have SRI funds with different restriction levels to choose from.

Social investment funds and social-impact investing still provide financial returns, but the return expectation is lower. This type of investing fuels social entrepreneurship. The best-known social entrepreneur investment is probably microlending, which is frequently targeted at overseas development. Although microlending appeals to socially responsible investors, it can have drawbacks unless it is run well, by a good organization. Do some research before you invest.

A more local and trackable option for social-impact investing is to contribute to loans through Community Development Financial Institutions (CDFIs). This is a certification given to localized banks or credit unions, so you can find one near you. CDFIs provide credit and financial services to underserved markets and populations, often to community-based nonprofits for their local projects. CDFIs sometimes have microlending programs as well. You can invest by adding to the fund and getting a moderate return.

The Dynamic of Generosity and Interdependence

Two concepts underlie solidarity, justice giving, and spending. First, that your behavior as a giver occurs within a dynamic that includes the receiver and affects you both, beyond just a financial transaction. Second, that this interpersonal dynamic reflects a larger one, wherein we are all in some sense connected and reliant upon each other. This section will delve more deeply into the generative dynamic of giving and receiving and explore our shared connectedness using various definitions for the concept of interdependence. An understanding of giving within this dynamic relationship and broad conceptualization should better inform your philanthropic plan and, more broadly, your overall generosity.

The concept of interdependence is used prominently in at least two religious traditions: Buddhism and Unitarian Universalism. Buddhism teaches the concept of dependent origination: that nothing exists in isolation, independent of other life, and that all life is interrelated. According to dependent origination, bigness does not exist without smallness; without something small to compare it to, we would not know that something was big. The same can be said about good and evil or giving and receiving—they would not exist without each other. Dependent origination makes other Buddhist beliefs possible, such as the concept of *karma*, in which our actions create a cycle of cause and effect. These beliefs illustrate the concept of interdependence, where things exist separately from each other yet also affect each other in responsive

> And render to the kindred their due rights, as (also) to those in want, and to the wayfarer: but squander not (your wealth) in the manner of a spendthrift.
>
> The Qur'an

and dynamic ways. Causal interdependence is considered among the most important of Buddhist principles.[57]

Some of the interviewees considered their giving in light of this idea of cause and effect over time. Henry (p. 136) even used the Buddhist term when he said, "There were people who were generous to me and kind to me, and they are gone. So I am paying back through others who are in need. It is the concept of *karma*. I had a lot of that so I am trying to pay that back." Henry referred here specifically to financial generosity. Other people talked about doing good works now because they know that they will inevitably need help in the future.

Tom, who sees his current career success as being due in part to support he received from older mentors earlier in his career, extends this dynamic even further into the future. Having been a recipient not only spurs Tom to help currently; he also invests in the future by mentoring younger people to support their future achievements. He spends so much time on this that he said, "Sometimes this is difficult for my staff, but it is important to me."

Another Buddhist concept related to interdependence is that moral conduct benefits all beings one encounters, not just the person you hope to benefit directly through your actions or giving. To carry this line of thought to its conclusion, we are all connected and I am specifically, if indirectly, affected by what happens to a group of people anywhere on the planet. I am affected by what happens to you. So one reason to be philanthropic is that by my supporting *you* or *your* environment, no matter where that is located, I will ultimately make *my* world a better place to live. Elise spoke about how her personal giving can extend to benefit people beyond her personal sphere: "We are all interconnected. When I give to someone else or to causes, I believe that all of us benefit. My child benefits and future generations benefit."

Even more broadly, Anthony directly ties this inclusive effect to his giving behavior. He said, "What I give is so insignificant, yet by giving I am replicating the very energy I want to create in the universe."

The Unitarian Universalist religion has seven Principles as part of its primary guiding covenant. The concept of interdependence, which is expressed differently than in Buddhism, is described in the seventh of these principles: *Respect for the interdependent web of all existence, of which we are a part.* Although it is not limited to environmental concerns, this principle is almost always equated to our care for and place within the earth and its ecosystems, so it relates to scientific concepts of interdependence. Elise, who is a Unitarian Universalist, connects this concept of a web directly to her giving when she says, "I feel this interconnected web; if everyone pulled back on their web and held out into their little corner, then we would all just dry up. That sense of connectedness creates a broader benefit of my giving."

Rita (p. 26) is not a Unitarian Universalist, yet she expresses it similarly and with the image of a net, although from a more theistic perspective. Hers is an experience of an even larger "container" within which we all dwell—the abundance of creation:

> Everything we have has been given to us; everything that flows to us. We are just a vessel of a greater energy. These blessings are not ours, and we should pass them along. This world is the net we are living in—it is the spirit of God, energy, creation. God is a generous God.

It may be helpful here to note how scientifically modern the Unitarian Universalist seventh Principle is as a religious expression. Although Unitarian Universalism has its roots among Jewish and Christian sources, this idea is very different from the Biblical belief (Genesis 1:26, for instance) in man's *dominion* over the Earth and its contents. The idea that the natural world is human-centered and that the environment's purpose is to benefit humans has been evolving in some more traditional Christian theologies so that it is more ecologically based, and humans are seen as God's stewards of the environment. Yet, in traditional interpretation, the idea of human dominion is antithetical to interdependence and may have affected people's support of environmental causes. Despite its theological sources, the Unitarian Universalist use of interdependence in its seventh Principle is closely related to the way word is used in biology.

As a scientific term, *interdependence* means the relationship in which individuals within one species, or of different species living in a habitat, depend upon on each other. This is easily understood even by non-scientists through the concept of an ecosystem. When applied to human relationships, the dynamic of giving and receiving is part of how we sustain each other and build social networks. Anthony took care of a friend's wife as she died of cancer. He said this taught him that "This is the pattern of life; there is being cared for, and there is caring for others."

Most of this book's stories and interviews illustrate the building and deepening of mutually dependent relationships through the dynamic of giving and receiving. Studies show that prosocial spending—spending on other people or charitable gifts—contributes to building relationships.[58] Social connections like these produce many benefits. Reviews of hundreds of research studies confirm that strong social connections increase survival;[59] and conversely, prolonged and enduring feelings of loneliness increase the risk of most age-related conditions such as heart disease, cancer, and Alzheimer's.[60] In the elderly, a strong network of friends has been linked to greater resilience, better mood, coping, and self-esteem.[61] Even happiness has been shown to increase with more social support.[62] Giving also increases happiness; studies demonstrate that when people benefit other people, they are measurably happier. Daniel (p. 70) cited the personal benefits he feels from giving: "I feel better about myself today because I am helping people. That is good for me. It is healthier for me. It is good for me spiritually."

Aside from these health and psychological benefits, personal giving relationships can provide opportunities for "feedback loops," wherein the dynamic of giving and receiving encourage and fuel each other. This motivation can occur out of having greater happiness as a result of giving. For example, if you receive support or a gift graciously, it can inform how you understand giving and receiving, both increasing your generosity and making you more open as a recipient. This kind of ever-evolving cycle is illustrated below:

Just as being more adept and gracious at receiving increases our ability to receive, giving can be a positive experience that motivates more giving. Behavioral research in the workplace, and even with children in religious situations, has found that happier people give more. Analysis of brain activity has also confirmed these effects.[63] Social research has affirmed the feedback loop effect, wherein happier people give more, get happier, and give even more.[64] This may be what Elise meant when she said, "By giving, we blossom ten-fold."

The life experiences of Anthony, Rita and Jim (p. 26), and Liz that are included in previous chapters helped them develop as receivers, to grow in their understanding of giving and receiving as parts of an interwoven and fluid dynamic. Giving and receiving cannot be separated; when one part increases, so does the other. When this dynamic is flowing well, something is created beyond what is given and received.

Gratitude also can be a vehicle to generate a feedback loop, where after receiving, one wants to give back. As Liz said, "I have been given so much that I didn't ask for or I didn't deserve. That is why I have to share it as much as possible and help other people to find what they should have."

This positive feedback loop also may be operating for Henry. Aside from his strategic giving and work in a nonprofit, he also gives a lot of care more casually. He helps people with their resumes, assists elderly neighbors, and loans people money. Henry has also looked after the daughter of a former colleague who has moved into his community to attend college. He has advised her, given her money, and even bailed her out of some personally challenging situations. Henry said,

> I get a lot of great feedback from people that I help. I feel needed, appreciated, wanted. I like to get acknowledged and they are very grateful and appreciative. In turn, they are kind to me, which makes me feel good.

Many people have realized that an understanding of the interdependent nature of giving and receiving provides feelings of freedom and confidence, which can motivate further giving. This comes with knowing that you can give generously, not only because you trust that you will be able to earn, create, or find more of whatever you give away. It also grows your belief in the web of social connectedness where others will step in to help or support you when you need it. Reducing your anxiety about the future, about your capabilities, what you might need, and even what you might have to give is motivating. It allows you to risk stepping into new activities, deeper levels of relationship, and more engagement with the world.

Liz said she actually gains more than she gives in this work: "The insights are phenomenal in terms of the richness of experiences and relationships with people. From a generosity perspective, I always feel that I get so much more than I give."

Interdependence in the sciences—from quantum physics exploring the tiniest units of matter, to medicine's study of the human body, to astronomy's study of distant planets—brings us to greater levels of understanding about how we humans and everything else are all connected. Brad speaks passionately and eloquently about this in practical terms:

> You can't separate yourself from the rest of the world. If anything goes wrong in one part of the world, it's going to affect the United States. The odds are that people will be displaced, that's one thing. A certain percentage of them would like to come here and a certain number get here. U.S. interests are connected to the interests everywhere and if someone has tuberculosis and wanders around, you are apt to get it.

Indeed, a war in the Middle East affects everyone on this planet. The suffering and loss of life on both sides of any conflict are tragically obvious. Environmental damage caused by war in one country will affect even the most pristine area in a far distant part of Earth. Negative economic effects from violent conflict are felt well beyond any war zone (the sales of arms notwithstanding). These include the interruption of supply chains, the destruction of commerce sources such as crops and factories, and the displacement of workers. War creates a refugee population that strains the resources of neighboring countries. Politically, there is seldom a strong action anywhere in the world that does not create a reaction in other parts of the world. Here is how Brad expressed it:

> Right now, my motto is "We live in an irrevocable, interconnected, Internet world, with problems that no country can solve alone." We are all world citizens. The fact that we are here with all of the other people on Earth is unavoidable today.

Interdependence has been used in other realms as well. In 1944, the Pulitzer Prize-winning philosopher Will Durant published a "Declaration of Interdependence" to promote racial equity through appealing for human tolerance, fellowship, mutual consideration, and respect.[65] Since then, documents given that same title have addressed growing loving relationships, cooperative economies, peacemaking, and interreligious respect. Recently, the filmmaker Tiffany Shlain promoted humanity as a global community by writing a "Declaration of Interdependence," putting the script on the web, and gathering video footage submissions from whoever wanted to submit them.[66] She then created and distributed the resulting montage. She made this available through an innovative video project, where her company will customize the film so even very small nonprofits can use it for their own fundraising purposes. More than one hundred nonprofit organizations have participated so far. There is even an organization that supports a yearly international Day of Interdependence[67] on September 12.

Being willing to live more interdependently will make a difference in all the ways discussed in this chapter. When you give and receive care, you build relationships and improve your health and well-being. You can build your relationships, grow communities, and even mature as an individual. With your financial gifts, you can experience generative feedback loops fueled by mutual care, happiness, gratitude, and feelings of greater freedom and confidence. This knowledge should inform your philanthropic planning and incidental giving decisions, hopefully making them more bold and ambitious. Finally, believing in and embracing our interdependence can support efforts to make our societies more just through multiple lenses. As Liz affirmed,

> I believe people can do good for each other; we can make that difference. We have our destiny in our own hands, individually and collectively, and I think we should make that a destiny of helping as many people as possible.

The activity of planning, and the plan itself, are vital elements of developing your generosity. Throughout this book, you have been creating and gathering elements you can use in your plan. Articulating, recording, and committing to implement your plan are the best ways to ensure that you are more thoughtful and strategic in your giving. Amy-Lee, who was in the thick of her planning endeavor when I interviewed her, is a zealous advocate for financial and philanthropic planning. She expresses it this way:

> Money is not just about saving and spending on yourself; you have to use it too—for a purpose. Planning will help people with that. We have choices to make and have to plan so that everything is in order and we know what we can give. Then it becomes exciting.

As you start considering your plan, with an eye toward exercising and developing your generosity, it is vital that it is both ambitious and sustainable. Setting this balance is a challenge. This initial plan could be modest as a reflection of your current resources, stage of life, or a particular situation. Here Daniel recommends that, even if you are already busy, just a little bit will help others:

> If I was talking to someone who is a parent and has a job, I would say take stock and talk about choices that are available. What can you do financially or time-wise, even in a small way? You can always do something. If you find a group that you want to support financially, do you also have an hour once a month?

For others the plan might be extensive. Understand your plan as a document that probably will change on a regular basis. Your resources and priorities might shift, requiring a revision of the plan. In the longer term, there might be more profound changes in your contributions and where or how they are allocated.

Everyone's life contains uncertainties. You develop your philanthropic plan within the larger consideration of financial planning and budgeting. When considering your near or more distant financial future, try to be optimistic. For instance, preparing your plan for the collapse of the Social Security system, or a severe and expensive illness, will cause you to overestimate the financial resources you might need in the future. If you see a financial planner for assistance, understand that part of their job is to help provide you with as much buffer as possible. Your planner might not be educated about charitable giving, and so may not normally orient future plans toward generosity. You will have to bring that to the agenda!

While you are making these plans, remember the lessons you have learned in your own life about being a recipient, and about how the dynamic of giving and receiving can be generative and build relationships. Your plan should prepare reasonably and be mindful of the fact that no amount of money will prepare us for every eventuality. Even vast wealth will not avert the need to accept care from others. However, even as you remain mindful of the inevitable, you should not avoid the involvement of others in your support and care. If you are not stockpiling for every imaginable eventuality, you may be able to afford to be more ambitious than you think. In the end, I hope you will remember that your giving, whether modest or substantial, will help to create a more just and humane world for us all to live in.

Once you have completed the plan, use it immediately and often. Keep it where you can easily refer to it when making charitable gifts, and periodically review it. It may need a revision in the future as your circumstances change.

PRACTICES

Plan for Philanthropy
On the following page, you will find the format for a plan to practice generosity. It relies on the mission statement you created in chapter 3, your current budget (including current charitable giving) and your gifts and strengths from chapter 6, consideration of your core community and opportunities for communal giving from chapter 7, the research you did into nonprofits and strategy options from chapter 8, and your consideration of broader contexts and dynamics included in this chapter. The plan combines the causes you care about with the organizations that address those concerns, and then asks you to list how much volunteer and financial resource you want to commit. This may take you some time, and you may have to consult with a spouse or dependent before you can complete this plan. Take your time, and don't forget to include ways that you are already giving!

Journaling
Reflect on what you personally gain and value from giving. Try to think of at least one example of giving to a nonprofit organization, one instance of spontaneous giving, and one instance of giving to a community where you are involved in some ongoing effort.

- How do you describe the deeper benefit you gained? What indicators did you have of that benefit? Was there a particular place in your body, where you felt it?
- Did you benefit in any other ways that you noticed? For instance, did it affect how you approached another similar situation? Or did it allow you to step in and help to change a situation that was not going well?
- Reflect on what someone who gave you something may have gained in that process. Think of a particular instance of receiving a gift. What effect do you think the giving and your response had on them? If you can identify an effect, how did you know (an expression, something they said, a difference in mood you could sense)?

SOLIDARITY, JUSTICE GIVING, AND INTERDEPENDENCE

My Plan for Philanthropy

This format is a suggestion about to what to include in your plan. Do not let it limit your generosity. If it does not provide enough room, feel free to add a sheet or write on the back.

Name:	
Date:	
My personal mission statement:	
The causes, issues, populations I care about:	1. 2. 3. 4.
The organizations, groups, or people who are addressing the above:	1. 2. 3. 4.
The personal gifts and skills I have to offer the world:	1. 2. 3. 4.

How I want to use my gifts and skills (describe):	
My opportunities for giving collectively in a community, giving circle, or my family:	
Amount of time I will dedicate to make a difference (each week, month or year):	

Specific time blocks in my calendar (daily, weekly, monthly) that I will dedicate:

My intention for spontaneously giving my time, gifts, and skills:

The financial resources I have to work with (income minus responsibilities):		From ready cash and regular paychecks:	From savings, to to investments, possessions:	
Specific financial gifts I will give to this organization, group, or person:	Each $Amt Month	Each $Amt Year	Planned $Amt Gift*	
	1.	1.	1.	
	2.	2.	2.	
	3.	3.	3.	
	4.	4.	4.	
	5.	5.	5.	

My intention for spontaneously giving my financial resources:

* A planned gift is any major gift, made in a donor's lifetime or at death as part of a donor's overall financial and/or estate planning

Afterword

Because this book has covered a broad reach of material—from your personal understanding of your role as a financial giver, to concrete information about resources for nonprofit research, to data on economic disparity—a brief review may be worthwhile, in addition to a few final pieces of key information to leave you with.

This book has reflected on ways in which you are already generous and about the opportunities you might find in your everyday life, no matter your life circumstance. In the first section about generosity, we considered how the definitions and meanings of wealth, poverty, and generosity are learned, and found new meaning in the word *philanthropy*. We looked at receiving as an important and challenging part of the dynamic of generosity. We identified the ways people learn about generosity and how we might teach others.

In the second section about practice, we considered the path of development, which is supported by gratitude; we explored both daily and long-term development. We examined the risks and barriers to being generous, including self-limiting fears we may have about our future. We explored how our own vibrancy enables our giving to others, sustaining that energy and accounting for our finances.

We also explored how communities can provide practice, mentors, examples, and colleagues in generosity, as well as the things that inhibit and invite generosity in a community context.

Because our generosity is often directed toward nonprofits or community groups, we took a look at how fundraising works, at the items used to garner donations—and at deeper, richer benefits that we might seek. We also examined starting strategies and tools for skillful giving. The current conditions of economic stratification were presented as a frame to consider solidarity, a multicultural approach, and justice giving and spending as ways to foster kinship. Finally, we looked at the potential of giving and receiving to produce interdependence and generative dynamics; we considered these as ways to help prepare a philanthropic plan.

> Generosity is about being free. The generous are free from the things of this world. While they own possessions, their possessions do not own them. They are free from taking for their own benefit and are free to give, even when it results in personal sacrifice. Generosity is love in action, and love is measured in giving, not taking.
>
> Erwin Raphael McManus

Three areas of exploration emerged as central themes of this book. The first addresses the deeper benefits people gain from being generous. The second covers how people learn about and become generous. The third concerns community giving and what that can mean, both for individual members and for the group.

Regarding the benefits of generosity, we may ask, simply: What rewards keep people stepping into generosity over and over again? In the personal stories of the interviewees, we see that being generous helps these people:

- connect with others and create community
- support their identity as a mature or good person
- find meaning and purpose in their lives
- build solidarity and kinship across economic divisions
- align values, beliefs, and loves with resources and actions
- experience good feelings.

Regarding how people learn to be generous, the interviews reveal a pattern for how generosity develops. This is particularly useful in thinking about how we might impart generosity to others, both adults and kids. The interviewees presented vastly different personal histories, yet all of them led to people who were very generous. Most of them described a two-stage process of learning, first in a formative way during childhood and then developing that learning in adulthood through a number of means. By identifying how generous people learned generosity, we can draw conclusions about ways to teach it. These ways of teaching include:

1. Giving direct guidance and instruction in sharing resources, allocating money toward charitable giving, or refusing pay for volunteer work.
2. Acting as role models by openly acting in generous ways, discussing giving plans, and volunteering.
3. Exposing people to others who are disadvantaged or to issue areas (such as environmental degradation), so they see and have some first-hand understanding.
4. Engaging people with experience by inviting them to participate in meaningful volunteering or connected donorship.
5. Being available as mentors; cultivating guiding relationships with people who are less experienced.
6. Creating and/or inviting people to join a community of practice, so people can find kinship in the development and practice of generosity.

Most of the people interviewed experienced a combination of these ways to learn. Some had one type of instruction in one phase of life and another in a second phase; others benefited from a combination at the same time in their life. In the end, there is no telling what will create an epiphany or tipping point for people, yet when it does happen, the methods listed above probably contributed to it. We might learn a couple of things from this. First, although a good family culture about being charitable is helpful, you can still develop generosity later in life. Second, our life experiences, both tragic and delightful, can be a vehicle for growing in generosity. A community of practice can serve as a platform where all the other ways of learning can be made available.

Regarding building communities of practice, most nonprofits, religious organizations, giving circles, and other charitable organizations have at least two purposes aside from just running their organizations:

1. implementing programs toward their mission goals
2. engaging and building community support to carry their message and to obtain volunteers and financial fuel.

There is another purpose, although many do not take advantage of it:

3. provide a setting to practice generosity, incorporating most or all of the ways of learning listed above: a community of practice.

These must be offered in an authentic and non-self-serving way, for the benefit of the member, in a way that builds kinship.

The potential for this work is profound. I am inspired by the wisdom of Arturo Paoli, an Italian missionary priest who lived and worked, until his very old age, among the poorest people of Venezuela. He has written in very critical ways about globalization and the world economy. Yet he has also come to understand money as having the ability to join us together in community, and to distribute justice. Rather than money being symbolic of privilege and power, Paoli believes that money can be a symbol of life and of justice. He has even reportedly expressed that money can be like grace, used as a means for individuals to exchange goodness. To me this recasting of money as a tool of justice and a vehicle for care is creative, inspiring, and useful.

People who are considerate, present for receiving, and willing to give at any moment are rare—they resonate with our deepest desires. Others feel a kinship and are drawn to them, not because they want to take advantage, but because the generous people are a refuge from the challenges that separate us. They make people feel seen and heard. They are examples and inspirations, providing hope and a way forward. When you are around them, they seem deeply satisfied, even fulfilled. I can feel these possibilities in myself and in my own relationships. Perhaps you have gotten a glimmer of them in yourself as you worked through the book. If so, continue developing your generosity so you can fully realize this way of being.

If the challenges set out in this book seem overwhelming, do not be discouraged. Give yourself time to open up your generosity, slowly and in your own way. If you are patient with yourself and accept your own limitations (until you can change them!), this experience will be easier and more enjoyable. Remember, all your efforts are built on the stable foundation of your generosity to yourself. Your expectations of what you can do, and of the organizations and people you hope to benefit, should be reasonable and possible. Take your time, as gradually you will learn more and more about what it means to be generous.

Thank you for joining me on this path into generosity. I continue to challenge my own generosity every day. As I look to the future, it does not always appear easy. Yet each of the people who shared their stories in the preceding chapters described the benefits they felt and the challenges they faced, no matter how matter-of-fact or effortless they may seem in retrospect. This path is so countercultural, it cannot be achieved quickly or ever finalized; it may last until our final hour.

So here our paths diverge. I wish you well on your journeys from here. Blessings on your way!

PRACTICES

Revisit the Start

Go back to the Generosity Self-Assessment you completed at the beginning of this book (p. 16). Also go back to the letter to yourself from the future you wrote at the end of chapter 1 (p. 14). You can review all of your journal entries to get a picture of the path you have taken so far, and the changes you have noticed. Spark your curiosity with these questions:

- How has my thinking and approach changed during the time of reading this book?
- Have I become more present to receiving? Have I become a more thoughtful giver?
- What pieces have been particularly challenging? Has any of that work been left undone?
- Has my thinking changed about my role and purpose during this time?

Journaling

Reflect on these questions, or others you think are relevant:

What new path do I want to set for myself from here?

How do I want to shift my vision from the letter to myself; what elements still fit?

What efforts do I plan to undertake to build kinship and join in solidarity with others?

What is the next level of development for me?

For Further Reading

There are many books available about how to use money to better ourselves and the world; this is a brief list to get you started on further reading.

Blanchard, Ken, and S. Truett Cathy. *The Generosity Factor: Discover the Joy of Giving Your Time, Talent, and Treasure.* Zondervan, 2002.

Clark, Wayne B. *Beyond Fundraising: A Complete Guide to Congregational Stewardship.* Unitarian Universalist Association of Congregations, 2007.

Clinton, Bill. *Giving: How Each of Us Can Change the World.* Knopf, 2007.

Dominguez, Joe, and Vicki Robin. *Your Money or Your Life.* Penguin Books, 2008.

Gary, Tracy, and Melissa Kohner. *Inspired Philanthropy: Your Step-By-Step Guide to Creating a Giving Plan.* 3rd edition. Jossey-Bass, 2008.

Haughey, John C., S.J. *Virtue and Affluence: The Challenge of Wealth.* Sheed & Ward, 1997.

Hyde, Lewis. *The Gift: Imagination and the Erotic Life of Property.* Random House, 1979.

Jamal, Azim, and Harvey McKinnon. *The Power of Giving: How Giving Back Enriches Us All.* Jaico Publishing, 2006.

Karoff, Peter. *The World We Want: New Dimensions in Philanthropy and Social Change.* AltaMira Press, 2006.

————. *Just Money: A Critique of Contemporary American Philanthropy.* TPI Editions, 2004.

Kass, Amy A., ed. *The Perfect Gift: The Philanthropic Imagination in Poetry and Prose.* Indiana University Press, 2002

Needleman, Jacob. *Money and the Meaning of Life.* Doubleday, 1994.

Salamon, Julie. *Rambam's Ladder: A Meditation on Generosity and Why It Is Necessary to Give.* Workman Publishing, 2003.

Sider, Ronald J. *Just Generosity: A New Vision for Overcoming Poverty in America*, 2nd ed. Baker Books, 2007.

Toycen, Dave. *The Power of Generosity: How to Transform Yourself and Your World.* Authentic/Om Literature, 2004

Twist, Lynne. *The Soul of Money: Reclaiming the Wealth of Our Inner Resources.* W.W. Norton & Co, 2003.

Vardey, Lucinda, and John Dalla Costa. *Being Generous: The Art of Right Living.* Alfred A. Knopf, 2007.

For Kids

Dyer, Wayne W. *It's Not What You've Got!: Lessons for Kids on Money and Abundance.* Hay House, Inc. 2007.

Gallo, Eileen, and Jon J. Gallo. *Silver Spoon Kids: How Successful Parents Raise Responsible Children.* Contemporary Books, 2002.

Maestro, Betsy. *The Story of Money.* HarperCollins, 1995.

Otfinoski, Steven. *The Kid's Guide to Money: Earning It, Saving It, Spending It, Growing It, Sharing It.* Scholastic, 1996.

Roehlkepartain, Eugene C., Elanah Dalyah Naftali, and Laura Musegades. *Growing Up Generous: Engaging Youth in Giving and Serving.* Alban Institute, 2000.

Weisman, Carol. *Raising Charitable Children.* F. E. Robbins & Sons Press, 2006.

Zeiler, Freddi. *A Kids Guide to Giving.* InnovativeKids, 2006.

Small Group Discussion Guide

For the Facilitators

First of all, thank you for convening and leading this group. This guide is meant to support you and your members; please be as flexible with it as necessary. It is structured according to the book chapters, so you might schedule eleven meetings, the first an introduction and the last a celebration, review, and closing. The length of each meeting will depend on how many members you have. If your group has more than twelve people, it will be best to break into smaller groups for the discussion segments, then bring everyone back together periodically to share highlights. Take all the time you need for each subject that you consider. It is far better to cover one topic completely than to skim over many topics, without deep reflection. Remember that everyone has the right to be heard, and also can choose to remain quiet on any topic.

Whether you are facilitating this group as an individual or co-leader, the group members will look to you to be a model of generosity in the way you conduct the group. Do not let this pressure weigh you down! The best way for you to "show up" is as your authentic self. This means that you should exercise your prerogative to make mistakes and apologize and to be fallible, incorrect, and generally human. That way, you model an authentic grappling with the topic rather than personal brilliance on the subject.

Depending on how the group is meant to function, it may help to read the entire book and do all of the practices and journaling yourself before facilitating the group. If it is a more self-led group, you can rotate the facilitator role and all move through the book together.

Ask participants to bring their journals to each meeting, as they might be useful both as a reference and for writing in during the meeting. You may decide to build in some time during each group meeting for participants to record their reflections or ideas.

This guide follows the general outline of the chapters and uses group activities to find commonalities, embrace differences, and build mutual support. Hopefully, this will help to build a community of practice for you and your group members. To make that more possible, use a gentle and non-judgmental approach (see Chapter 7 for more on communities of practice).

Small group activities correspond to the contents of each of the chapters. It is suggested that you do one of these (or something like it) at the beginning of your meeting and allow some time to discuss the activity afterward. The provided discussion questions can help get the conversation going. You can ask one question or a number of them. Once the discussion is going, it is only necessary to step in if the conversation has strayed too far from the subject or the discussion peters out.

Small Group Activities for Each Chapter

Introductory Meeting

Ask each participant to introduce themselves. Depending on the number of participants, and how well they already know each other, determine the length of the introductions by requesting specific types of information (name, how long involved with convening organization or convener, past experience with others in group, pertinent biographical info, etc.).

Next, invite each participant to respond as they wish to these two questions:

- What path brought you here?
- What are you hoping to gain from participating in this group, reading the book together, or from being more generous?

You may also want to make an agreement about how you want to be together as a group—including confidentiality, how the meetings will be conducted, and communication within the group; this is sometimes called a *covenant*. You can also review the number of meetings you plan to hold and the proposed topics for each of them. Make sure group members have each other's phone numbers and email addresses.

Chapter 1: Starting Where You Are

Wallet Exercise and Introductions:
Have everyone sit in a circle.

Ask participants to take out their wallet, or whatever they carry money and charge cards in. Have each person pass their wallet to the person sitting to their left, then pass to the left again. Have them sit with the other's wallet for a few minutes, then ask people to introduce themselves. As part of the introduction, ask them to say something about what it feels like to hold someone else's wallet or to have their wallet being held by someone else.

When the introductions are finished, make sure to ask if people have other reactions they would like to share.

Questions Related to the Chapter:
Look again at the bulleted list of thoughts you may have regarding generosity (p. 9). Do any of them resonate for you? If so, which ones? What about them applies to your circumstances?

Regarding the Generosity Self-Assessment:

- What did you learn about how you compare giving money and giving volunteer skills and time?

- What did you learn about how your self-care, care for others, and receiving care relate to each other?
- Were there any "a-ha" moments for you?

In the journaling exercise, you wrote a letter to yourself from your future self, five years from now. How did you picture your circumstances? How do those different circumstances support you in being more generous, or are you generous despite the circumstances you envisioned?

Chapter 2: The Generous Receiver

Stories of Receiving
Ask participants to pair up with partner whom they don't know very well.

Give them these instructions:

- Take a few minutes to think of a time when someone offered you tremendous generosity. It could have been a gift of time, intelligence, money, caring, or simply presence.
- Remember who that person was and what they gave you with as much detail as you can. Remember how you experienced that event and how it affected you afterward.
- Now, one at a time, tell your partner about the person who was generous to you and about the gift they gave you. You will each have about five minutes to tell the story.

Keep track of the time, telling the group when to switch to the next person talking and when to finish up. Then have the group come back together. Ask each person to introduce their partner to the group, sharing what they learned about their partner.

Questions Related to the Chapter:
- Have you ever been in a new environment (either overseas, like Liz (p. 174), or in the United States) where the cultural

ideas about giving and receiving were different? How did you discover the difference and what did you do?

- Think about a time when you were really uncomfortable with a gift you were given. Looking back, would you choose to react differently if you could? In what way?
- Have you ever really wanted something, and those around you knew it, yet no one gave it to you? How did you respond?
- Of all your "gifts" (strengths, attributes, qualities), are there any that you are uncomfortable sharing with those around you?

Chapter 3: Learning Generosity and Guiding Others

Pictures and Lessons

Prior to your meeting, ask participants to bring a photo of one or both parents, another loved one, a teacher, or mentor.

Have everyone sit in a circle. Ask each participant to introduce the people in their picture and share the lessons they learned from them that they use regularly in their current life. Make sure they include how these lessons were taught (instruction, modeling, working alongside them, mentoring, and so on). Then, invite each person to speak as they choose about how they have extended and enriched those lessons so they no longer do them just as they were taught.

Questions Related to the Chapter:

- What did you know about the financial giving of your family growing up?
- What do you remember about the families around you and their relative wealth?
- What indicators did you get of that level? How did you know?
- Is your current economic status different than it was then? If so, how?
- What do you think is the most effective way to teach financial generosity or to encourage people to give?

Chapter 4: Generosity as a Practice

Admiration Stories

Gather the group in a circle. Ask participants to identify some-one that they really admire (it can be someone else in the group). Have them picture the person and remember some interactions with them. Then have everyone, going around the circle, share the name of the person they admire and tell a brief story illustrating why they admire them. Encourage people not to just name quali-ties but to actually tell a story. Make sure to take a minute or two between each person speaking to let each story sink in.

Once everyone is done, have a discussion about where generos-ity is found in the stories. What parts of the stories related to the person's regularity or constancy in giving?

Questions Related to the Chapter:
- How do your values or religious beliefs inform your giv-ing and receiving?
- Are there intersections between your regular spiritual practices and generosity (giving and receiving)?
- What everyday practices for giving do you have in place? How did you determine those; did they just evolve natu-rally, or with intention?
- What opportunities do you have to express your grati-tude? Where and with whom are those opportunities available? How regularly can that happen?
- In recent days, have you shifted your reaction in a stress-ful situation to be more generous?

Chapter 5: Risks and Barriers

Overflowing Hands

In advance of the meeting, gather as many coins as you can in a large bag, and bring them to the meeting. If you have a co-facilita-tor, ask that person to bring coins as well.

Once everyone is gathered in a circle, ask the participants to be completely silent and put their hands face-up in front of them, forming a cup. Then go around and fill each person's hands to overflowing with the coins. Make sure there is enough for everyone in the group—which means you may need to go around a few times until all the coins have been used (some will spill onto the ground!).

When everyone's hands are overly full of coins, ask the participants to stand and greet each other with as much warmth as they normally would.

Collect the coins again (or offer that they can keep them!) and ask everyone return to their seats to respond to the exercise. If people do not start discussing immediately, you can ask some questions:

- What was it like to have more coins than you could handle? Was it exciting, silly, or did it seem like a waste of money?
- Have you ever had more money than you could handle? Most people have not. If it has never happened to you, what would it be like to have more money than you can use? Can you even imagine that?
- What happened when you tried to greet other people with your hands full? Were you able to work it out together? Was it impossible?
- Did you want to keep the coins, or was it important to return them to the person who brought them?

Questions Related to the Chapter:
- Aside from time constraints, what other barriers to generosity affect you in your daily life?
- When you consider being your most generous, what are you concerned will happen as a result?
- Have you ever given away something that you valued, when you did not intend to give it—or gave more than you felt comfortable giving? How do you think about that incident now?

- How would your family, friends, and colleagues respond if you stated that you were going to focus a lot of your attention on ways to be more generous? Who do you know who would be excited and supportive of your intention?

Chapter 6: Developing and Sustaining the Giver

Receiving Practice

Break the group into pairs. Have participants sit facing each other directly, knee to knee. Provide all the instructions for the exercise at the outset; then while it is underway, walk the participants through, step by step.

Provide these instructions:

1. Gaze at each other softly, without searching or trying to convey anything with your eyes.
2. Take a deep breath together, then another. Breathe normally together.
3. After you are settled and comfortable, one person says to the other:
   "I recognize the spark of the divine in you." (note: you can adjust the language to "great spirit" or "beauty")
4. The receiver does not speak —just takes this in, focusing on receiving.
5. Take a deep breath together, then another.
6. Switch roles and go through the process again, with the person who was the receiver doing the speaking.

Gather the group back together and discuss what was experienced by the giver (who did not get a verbal "thank you") and the receiver (who was focused on receiving). Then continue the discussion, inviting participants to share as they are willing whether they are more comfortable as a giver or as a receiver, offering examples and stories from their lives to illustrate their preferences.

Questions Related to the Chapter:

- Think back on a time when you felt that you had everything you needed. What was sustaining you at that time?
- How do you fill yourself up (spirit, soul, energy), and how does that relate to giving to other people?
- What ways have you found to balance what you need with what others need?
- What things that do not cost money enrich you or give you a sense of well-being?
- Over the past week, have you seen an easy opportunity to be generous in a spontaneous way? Tell that story.

Chapter 7: Communities of Generosity

Growing Communities

Note: If all participants are from the same community or organization (such as a religious congregation or denomination, a community group, or a nonprofit) you will need to conduct this activity a little differently than if the group has formed from diverse place. Adapt as necessary.

Ask participants to identify the place that serves as their "core community." This could be a religious organization, their neighborhood, or a community group (such as Toastmasters, a food co-op, Rotary, a nonprofit volunteer corps, political party, hobby group, etc.).

Distribute two sets of Post-it Notes to everyone in the group. Each person should end up with three or four yellow Post-its and three or four white ones.

Give everyone about five minutes to write on their notes:

- One word on each of the *yellow* notes that describes what that core community provides for them. What benefits do you gain from being part of that community? How does it support or improve your life?
- One word on each of the *white* notes that describes what that core community offers to the surrounding world.

What opportunities does it offer to anyone who arrives? What activities does it do to serve the surrounding locality?

Then, have everyone post them on the wall. Ask them to organize the notes, categorizing the benefits in clusters (regardless of paper color). Ask the group to name each cluster, then write the name on a Post-it Note, and label the cluster.

Next, lead a discussion based on the question:

How can each of us grow those benefits and offerings?

Ask a volunteer to record everything and send it out to the group.

Questions Related to the Chapter:
- Give an example of a time when you gave your money, time, intelligence, and skills all to the same organization. How is that different from just giving money?
- Do you feel that your financial support is essential to any organization or person?
- How do you think your giving relates to what others give? What information informs your thinking?
- In your community, is there someone you look to as an exemplar of financial generosity?
- How does your community ask for contributions from people who have different abilities to give? Are there ways that might be improved?

Chapter 8: Being a Skillful Donor and Strategies for Your Philanthropic Plan

Show and Tell

Ask participants to bring a communication piece (mailer, brochure, newsletter, magazine) from a charitable organization that they support, either financially, through volunteering, or in both ways. It can be something from the person's core community or from another community. Bring a few extra that people can use if they forget theirs.

Ask the group to take a few minutes to reflect on what their connection (or disconnection) to this organization means to them. Then, invite each person to introduce the organization to the group, even if everyone knows it, using the communication piece. As part of the introduction, they should include the deeper benefits that can be gained by supporting this organization.

Questions Related to the Chapter:
- Do you budget separately for your charitable giving, or is it part of your overall spending plan?
- Do you give to anyone (person, group, or organization) on a regular basis, year after year? If so, how is that different for you than giving one time or irregularly?
- Have you ever been frustrated in trying to make a gift to an organization because they refused your gift, or because it did not work out? What did you learn from that situation?
- What kind of donor benefits have you received? Were they things you valued?
- Do you prefer to give lots of small gifts, on a regular basis, or a few larger gifts less frequently? How did you determine that preference?

Chapter 9: Solidarity, Justice Giving, and Interdependence

Four Quotes
In advance of the meeting, write the following four quotations on large sheets of paper. Before everyone arrives, post them on each of the four walls of the room where you are meeting.

- "Those of us who have grown in true love know that we can love only in proportion to our capacity for independence."—Fred Rogers (Mister Rogers)

- "We are here to awaken from the illusion of our separateness." —Thich Nhat Hanh
- "Every single instance of a friend's insincerity increases our dependence on the efficacy of money." —William Shenstone
- "We are all in the same boat, in a stormy sea, and we owe each other a terrible loyalty." —G.K. Chesterton

Ask participants to stand near the quotation that they resonate with the most. Give everyone a few minutes to talk to the others who are also standing near that quotation.

Bring the group back together, and invite participants to share about why they chose their particular quotation.

Questions Related to the Chapter:
- Have you ever had a close relationship with someone from a different socioeconomic level? Were there challenges related to money in that relationship?
- If your socioeconomic level has changed from what it was in the past, what have you noticed about how that affected your personal relationships? Your giving?
- How does or might your family approach giving together? What resources have been helpful to you in doing that?
- In the future, if you need to rely on someone's help, where do you think that assistance will come from?
- What strategies are at the forefront of your planning? What led you to that approach?

Closing Meeting

Appreciation Hands
Hand out blank pieces of 8½ x 11-inch paper to everyone, along with pens, crayons, or markers.

Split the group into pairs and have them sit together. Ask for silence during the activity. Conduct the activity in this manner:

- Ask each participant to trace the hand of their partner onto the paper, and write the partner's name on it. The person doing the tracing should hold onto the drawing of their partner's hand.
- Ask the person who drew the tracing to write something they appreciate or admire about their partner inside one of the five fingers of the tracing—and hold onto the drawing.
- Come back together in the larger group.
- Have each person pass the drawing they are holding to the person next to them (*not* the person whose name is on the drawing).
- Now ask the person holding the drawing to write something they appreciate or admire on the inside of the hand outline, about the person named on the paper.
- Keep going until everyone has written on everyone else's drawing.
- Give the pictures to the people whose names are on them.

Notes

1   Elizabeth W. Dunn, Lara B. Aknin, Michael I. Norton, "Spending Money on Others Promotes Happiness," *Science* (March 21, 2008).
2   Ibid.
3   Jonathan Gruber, "Pay or Pray? The Impact of Charitable Subsidies on Religious Attendance," *Journal of Public Economics* (2002).
4   Keely S. Jones, "Giving and Volunteering as Distinct Forms of Civic Engagement," *Nonprofit and Voluntary Sector Quarterly* (2006).
5   Bastian Hartmann and Martin Werding, "Donating Time or Money: Are They Substitutes or Complements?" *CESifo Working Paper: Behavioural Economics* (2012).
6   Mark O. Wilhelm, Eleanor Brown, Patrick M. Rooney, and Richard Steinberg, "The Intergenerational Transmission of Generosity," *Journal of Public Economics* (2008).
7   Parker J. Palmer, in an interview by Mark Nepo for the Fetzer Institute (2003), http://learningtogive.org/resources/folktales/interviews/Parker_Palmer.asp.
8   Eileen Gallo and Jon J. Gallo, *Silver Spoon Kids: How Successful Parents Raise Responsible Children* (Contemporary Books, 2002).
9   Robert A. Emmons and Michael E. McCullough, eds., *The Psychology of Gratitude* (Oxford University Press, 2004).
10 Joan Halifax, interview with Krista Tippett, "On Being," National Public Radio broadcast, 2013.
11 Bill Gates, Commencement Speech, 2007, Harvard University, Cambridge, MA.
12 John A. Buehrens, *Universalists and Unitarians in America: A People's History* (Skinner House Books, 2011). Note: Young's religious affilia-

tion was Universalist.

13 Adrienne Rich, "Natural Resources," in *The Dream of a Common Language: Poems 1974–1977* (W. W. Norton & Co. Inc., 1978).

14 Duke Helfand, "The Boundaries of Generosity," *Los Angeles Times*, April 30, 2008.

15 Eric Asimov, "Grapes and Power: A Mondavi Melodrama," *New York Times*, June 20, 2007.

16 Jack Knox, "Custodian an Honours Graduate of the School of Generosity," *Times Colonist Newspaper*, April 26, 2008.

17 Jennifer Stone, "New Business Owner Sees Generosity of Community," *Clarington This Week*, May 1, 2008.

18 Jean Lave and Etienne Wenger, *Situated Learning: Legitimate Peripheral Participation* (Cambridge University Press, 1991).

19 Paul Schervish and András Szántó, "Wealth and Giving by the Numbers," *Reflections: Excerpts from Wealth & Giving Forum Gatherings* (Wealth & Giving Forum, Fall 2006).

20 Julie Salamon, *Rambam's Ladder* (Workman Publishing Company, 2003).

21 Armin Falk, "Gift Exchange in the Field," *Econometrica* (August 3, 2007).

22 Tom Farsides and Sally Hibbert, "Charitable Giving and Donor Motivation" (National Council for Voluntary Organisations, 2005).

23 http://goodintents.org/aid-recipient-concerns/autisim-aspergers

24 http://goodintents.org/media-and-charitable-advertising/do-charity-fundraising-activities-hurt

25 www.hazelhenderson.com/2001/12/01/world-paper-better-than-b-1-bombers-and-pop-tarts-for-afghanistan-is-the-buckyball-way-of-thinking-by-hazel-henderson-commenting-from-st-augustine-fl-december-2001

26 Ernst Ferh and Collin F. Camerer, "Social Neuroeconomics: The Neural Circuitry of Social Preferences," *TRENDS in Cognitive Sciences* (Vol. 11, No. 10).

27 Elizabeth Dunn, Laura Aknin, and Michael Norton, M. I., "Spending Money on Others Promotes Happiness," *Science*, 319 (2008).

28 Stephanie L. Brown and R. Michael Brown, "Selective Investment Theory: Recasting the Functional Significance of Close Relationships," *Psychological Inquiry* (Vol. 17, No. 1, 2006).

29 James Andreoni, "Impure Altruism and Donations to Public Goods: A Theory of Warm-Glow Giving," *Economic Journal* (June, 1990).

30 Ron Jordan and Katelyn L. Quynn, *Invest in Charity: A Donor's Guide to Charitable Giving* (John Wiley & Sons, 2001).

31 www.cfp.net/utility/find-a-cfp-professional

32 Peter Singer, *The Life You Can Save: How to Do Your Part to End World Poverty* (Random House, 2010).

33 http://youtu.be/rypQL1zlzb0

34 www.communityfoundations.net

35 www.sarvodaya.org

36 John C. Haughey, SJ, *Virtue and Affluence: The Challenge of Wealth* (Sheed & Ward, 1997).

37 http://politicalcorrection.org/blog/201109130008

38 Emmanuel Saez and Thomas Piketty, "Income Inequality in the United States, 1913–1998," *The Quarterly Journal of Economics* (February 2003).

39 Markus Jäntti, et. al., *American Exceptionalism in a New Light: A Comparison of Intergenerational Earnings Mobility in the Nordic Countries, the United Kingdom and the United States* (Institute for the Study of Labor (IZA), 2006).

40 www.pewstates.org/research/reports/downward-mobility-from-the-middle-class-85899380141?p=1

41 www.pewstates.org/research/analysis/erin-currier-economic-mobility-and-the-american-dream-85899377180

42 Leonard Lopoo and Thomas DeLeire, *Pursuing the American Dream: Economic Mobility Across Generations* (The Pew Charitable Trusts, 2012).

43 www.pewsocialtrends.org/2012/01/11/rising-share-of-americans-see-conflict-between-rich-and-poor

44 http://philanthropy.com/article/Rich-Enclaves-Are-Not-as/133595

45 http://cgmf.org/blog-entry/15/Romney%27s-Empathy-Bypass-and-What-It-Means-for-Election-Day.html

46 http://philanthropy.com/article/America-s-Geographic-Giving/133591/

47 http://philanthropy.com/article/Rich-Enclaves-Are-Not-as/133595/

48 http://www.norc.org

49 Ash Amin, *The Social Economy: Alternative Ways of Thinking about Capitalism and Welfare* (Zed Books, 2009).

50 Paulo Freire, *Pedagogy of the Oppressed*, 30th Anniversary Edition (Continuum International Publishing Group, 2000).

51 John C. Haughey, *Virtue and Affluence: The Challenge of Wealth* (Sheed & Ward, 1997).

52 Margaret Oppenheimer and Nicholas Mercuro, *Law and Economics: Alternative Economic Approaches to Legal and Regulatory Issues* (M. E. Sharpe, Inc., 2004).

53 www.justiceharvard.org/resources/aristotle-the-politics

54 www.archives.gov/press/exhibits/dream-speech.pdf

55 http://leap-edu.org

56 www.classism.org/give-anonymously-give-openly

57 Masao Abe and Steven Heine, *Zen and the Modern World: A Third Sequel to Zen and Western Thought* (University of Hawaii Press, 2003).

58 Ed Diener and Martin E. P. Seligman, "Very Happy People," *Psychological Science* (January 2002).

59 Julianne Holt-Lunstad, Timothy B Smith, and J. Bradley Layton, "Social Relationships and Mortality Risk: A Meta-analytic Review." *PLOS Medical Journal* (July 2010).

60 Ibid.

61 Lynne C. Giles, Gary F. V. Glonek, Mary A. Luszcz, and Gary R. Andrews, "Effect of Social Networks on 10-Year Survival in Very Old Australians," *Journal of Epidemiological & Community Health,* 59 (2005).

62 Shawn Achor, *The Happiness Advantage: The Seven Principles of Positive Psychology That Fuel Success and Performance at Work* (Random House, 2010).

63 Lalin Anik, Lara B. Aknin, Michael I. Norton, and Elizabeth W. Dunn, *Feeling Good about Giving: The Benefits (and Costs) of Self-Interested Charitable Behavior* (Harvard Business School, 2009).

64 Ibid.

65 Ruth Wallach, Dace Taube, Claude Zachary, and Linda McCann, *Los Angeles in World War II* (Arcadia Publishing, 2011).

66 http://letitripple.org/a-declaration-of-interdependence

67 www.interdependencemovement.org